Skip the c3

The Grassroots Guide to Fiscal Sponsorship

By Tivoni Devor

Acknowledgments

I'd like to thank Kate Rivera, David Fair, and Andrew Shulman for their help in putting this guide together. I'd also like to thank my wife Jen, and daughter Ava for their help and support to get this book to you.

Copyright Tivoni Devor 2024, all rights reserved.

ISBN: 978-1-300-94937-4
Imprint: Lulu.com

Contents

Read this book before you sign a Fiscal Sponsorship Agreement 5
Part One: What is Fiscal Sponsorship 6
    What is Fiscal Sponsorship 6
    Professional vs. Casual Fiscal Sponsorship 7
        Professional Fiscal Sponsorship 7
        Casual Fiscal Sponsorship 8
    Models of Professional Fiscal Sponsorship 8
        Model A: Direct Project 9
        Model B: Independent Contractor Project 9
        Model C: Pre-Approved Grant Relationship 10
        Model D: Group Exemption 10
        Model E: Supporting Organization 10
        Model F: Technical Assistance 11
        Model L: Wholly Owned LLC 11
    Services Provided by Sponsors 11
        Nonprofit Entity Status Layer 12
    Legal Compliance Layer 13
    Back Office Layer 15
    The Cost of Fiscal Sponsorship 19
Part Two: Why Fiscal Sponsorship 20
    Is Fiscal Sponsorship Right for Your Vision? 20
    Who uses Fiscal Sponsorship and Why 22
        Short-term or temporary projects 22
        Startup organizations and pilot programs 23
        For-profits that want to do charitable activities: 24
        Established organizations: 24
        Foundations and Government Agencies: 25
    Myths of Fiscal Sponsorship 25

I will lose control of my organization. 25

This is just for startups. 26

It's expensive. 26

Risks of Fiscal Sponsorship 26

Part Three: Entering into a Fiscal Sponsorship Arrangement 29

What to ask when shopping for a Fiscal Sponsor 29

Fiscal Sponsorship Contract Negotiation 31

What the Fiscal Sponsor is going to ask for 32

What Fiscal Sponsors will say NO to 99% of the time. 34

INDEX 35

List of Fiscal Sponsors 35

Sample Applications 47

    The Community Foundation ████████████████ 47

    Center for ██████████ █████████ Leadership 55

    ████████ ████████ ████████ 60

    ████████ ████████ Community Foundation 64

    ███ ████████ 69

    The Foundation ████████ ████████ ████████ 77

Sample Agreements 87

    The ██████ Trust 87

    ██ Network 91

    ████████████ Alliance (CA) 102

    ████████████ ███████ Association (CT) 109

Other Fiscal Sponsorship Websites and resources 112

Read this book before you sign a Fiscal Sponsorship Agreement

I have worked at one of the United States's largest and oldest nonprofit providers of fiscal sponsorship services for over ten years. Over that time, I've spoken to over 1,000 nonprofit founders. Very few knew what Fiscal Sponsorship is, how it works, how the money is managed, and how power and authority are split between the provider of fiscal sponsorship and the founder looking for services.

I wrote this guidebook to help you and others become informed consumers of fiscal sponsorship. I've worked with many founders who are so excited and driven to launch their vision that they fail to read the Fiscal Sponsorship Agreement thoroughly, leading to mismatched expectations, money issues, hurt feelings, and damage to the mission.

Fiscal Sponsorship is one of those strange secrets of the nonprofit Industry; even though it has existed in one form or another for at least 50+ years, there are no laws or regulations about how Fiscal Sponsorship works. While there is a framework and best practices, which I share below, every organization that provides Fiscal Sponsorship does it differently.

Most nonprofit founders need access to lawyers to review the Fiscal Sponsorship agreement or deep knowledge of the nonprofit sector to understand the agreement and its implications, which puts them at a severe disadvantage when shopping for and signing a Fiscal Sponsorship Agreement.

Please use this book as a guide and reference on your Fiscal Sponsorship journey so that you will be better prepared to negotiate with your future Fiscal Sponsor.

Part One: What is Fiscal Sponsorship

What is Fiscal Sponsorship

In this section, I'll discuss why Fiscal Sponsorship may be the right choice for you. But first, let's make sure we understand what fiscal sponsorship is. Fiscal Sponsorship is when a 501c3 nonprofit organization allows you to use its legal entity and nonprofit status to cover you to accept tax-deductible donations, foundation grants, and government contracts—all necessary to fund the work you want to do. They are also legally responsible and liable for your work, the money you raise, the staff and volunteers you manage, and often the intellectual property you create.

Because your Fiscal Sponsor will, in most cases, be your legal entity of record and therefore responsible and entrusted with the money you raise and the work you do, in the event of a legal issue, they would be the organization getting sued (since your organization won't be a separate legal entity). Due to this risk, most Fiscal Sponsors will pay close attention to the legal liabilities and dangers associated with your work and the money you raise. Conversely, it would be best if you were very careful when choosing a Fiscal Sponsor because you have to trust them with your money—and yes, there have been times when bad Fiscal Sponsors have mismanaged funds or go out of business and take your money with them. In the third part of this book, I'll talk more about ensuring you pick a quality Fiscal Sponsor.

No specific laws or IRS regulations oversee the practice of Fiscal Sponsorship, so technically, anyone with 501c3 status can offer the use of their 501c3 to anyone else (although, in practice, it's better to work with an experienced Fiscal Sponsor). Because Fiscal Sponsorship isn't regulated (Fiscal Sponsors do, of course, still need to follow the same general legal and IRS guidelines that apply to all nonprofits), every Fiscal Sponsor does it differently—from services offered to the prices charged. This book will walk you through the many models and types of Fiscal Sponsorship practices and guide you through all the steps to set up a proper Fiscal Sponsorship agreement between you and the 501c3 you want to work with.

While various forms of Fiscal Sponsorship have been practiced for over 50 years, modern Fiscal Sponsorship was organized, modeled, and codified by Nonprofit Lawyer Gregory L. Colvin in 1993 when he published the book **Fiscal Sponsorship: Six Ways To Do It Right.** This book is considered the bible of Fiscal Sponsorship, and most professional Fiscal Sponsors use all the models he designed. Later in this book, we will dive into each of them (there are seven now) so you can choose the best model that works for your organization, and find a Fiscal Sponsor who provides that model of fiscal sponsorship.

Professional vs. Casual Fiscal Sponsorship

There are two levels of Fiscal Sponsorship providers. There are professional Fiscal Sponsors—nonprofits who focus on providing Fiscal Sponsorship as a service—and there are what I call casual Fiscal Sponsors. Casual Fiscal Sponsors offer Fiscal Sponsorship services as a favor or a side hustle. Still, it is not a core part of their mission, and they are often not operationally designed to provide the service or familiar with best practices.

Professional Fiscal Sponsorship

Professional Fiscal Sponsorship is provided by nonprofit organizations whose primary (or significant) focus is Fiscal Sponsorship. They may also do other types of work, but Fiscal Sponsorship is their main focus and area of expertise. Their operations are structured to provide this type of work, and they have staff dedicated to managing and supporting your Fiscal Sponsorship relationship. They will likely have a Fiscal Sponsorship application, review process, and contracts for you to sign; staff assigned to you, such as accountants, HR managers, and program support personnel; and will charge you fees, usually a percentage of the funds you raise. They are likely part of the National Network of Fiscal Sponsors and are listed on the Fiscal Sponsorship Directory.

Casual Fiscal Sponsorship

Usually, casual Fiscal Sponsorship is provided as a favor by a well-meaning organization looking to support a new project, and sometimes with a much smaller fee than professional Fiscal Sponsors. Casual Sponsorship is acceptable if you want to do short, simple projects or programs and have yet to pay staff or much money to manage. It can work for small community groups like a block fundraiser or a "Friends of the Local School" group. It is not suitable for a growing organization that may soon outgrow its casual Fiscal Sponsorship or need a level of service that the casual Fiscal Sponsor can't offer. It could even risk the casual Fiscal Sponsor's 501c3 status if your work is outside their mission and IRS classification.

Models of Professional Fiscal Sponsorship

There are seven generally recognized models of Professional Fiscal Sponsorship. These modern models of Fiscal Sponsorship were developed by nonprofit lawyer Gregory Colvin, who wrote the book on modern Fiscal Sponsorship: <u>Fiscal Sponsorship: 6 Ways to Do it Right</u> (Colvin Developed the 7th model after publishing his book). These models are usually followed by professional Fiscal Sponsors, but no laws or IRS regulations define Fiscal Sponsorship and its many models. While there are government regulations that cover nonprofits, the government has still not begun regulating Fiscal Sponsorship.

The seven modern models of Fiscal Sponsorship are:

- Model: A Direct Project
- Model B: Independent Contractor Project
- Model C: Pre-Approved Grant Relationship
- Model D: Group Exemption

- Model E: Supporting Organization
- Model F: Technical Assistance
- Model L: Wholly Owned LLC

Below, I briefly break down each one of these models. Models A, B, and C are the most commonly used types of fiscal sponsorship.

Model A: Direct Project

This is the most commonly used model and the one that I spend the most time discussing in this book. In this model, the entire project or organization you bring to a Fiscal Sponsor falls under their legal umbrella—they are the sole legal entity. This generally means that the Fiscal Sponsor will hold your funds, be the employer of record (hire staff), and be the default owner of any intellectual property your organization creates. The Fiscal Sponsor also bears full responsibility and liability for your actions. Their organization is legally on the hook in a lawsuit, not yours. You will sign a Fiscal Sponsorship agreement covering a scope of services (what services they will be offering you for the fee you pay) and details like how they will handle liability and intellectual property. The Fiscal Sponsor will charge a fee, typically 5% - 15% of your revenue. This model is good for both short-term and long-term projects and programs.

Model B: Independent Contractor Project

The independent contractor or project model is one where you have a legal entity that allows you to act as a subcontractor to the Fiscal Sponsor. This means that the Fiscal Sponsor outsources the work to your legal entity, which can be a for-profit like an LLC or an individual Sole Proprietor. This is mainly used for artists or individuals who can't receive nonprofit funds or grants directly, so they go through a Fiscal Sponsor. In this model, the artist writes the grants under the fiscal Sponsor's 501c3, and when they receive the grant, the

Fiscal Sponsor subcontracts with the artist or the artist's LLC to do that work. You then invoice the Fiscal Sponsor for payment. You will sign a Fiscal Sponsorship agreement covering a scope of services and details like how they handle liability and intellectual property. The Fiscal Sponsor will charge a fee between 5% and 15%. This model is good for individuals and short-term projects.

Model C: Pre-Approved Grant Relationship

This model is designed for newer projects or organizations that still need 501c3 status but want to apply for a specific grant. The fiscal Sponsor agrees only fiscally to sponsor you if you are awarded the grant. If you are not awarded the grant, you do not enter into a Fiscal Sponsorship relationship and should have to pay no fees. If awarded the grant, you enter into a Fiscal Sponsorship agreement, likely designed like Model A or B.

Model D: Group Exemption

The group exemption model is normally used for national organizations with local chapters, like the Boy Scouts and Girl Scouts, or any other large nonprofit with chapters in different locations. It allows the Chapters to use the National Organization's 501c3.

Model E: Supporting Organization

This is less used due to changes in IRS regulations but allows the project to file for their 501c3 but still be under the control of the Fiscal Sponsor.

Model F: Technical Assistance

This model is designed mostly for a Fiscal Sponsorship organization to provide fee-based technical assistance, consulting, and back-office services to independent 501c3s. Under this model, the Fiscal Sponsor is more of an advisor or service provider and does not have legal oversight over your organization.

Model L: Wholly Owned LLC

In this model, the Fiscal Sponsor creates a wholly-owned LLC for a specific project or program, intending to sell or spin off the LLC as a business unit. This is also used for projects that want to own real estate or situations where an LLC provides some distance between the Sponsor and the Project.

Services Provided by Sponsors

Every Fiscal Sponsorship provider is different. Each one may provide a different package of services and charge different rates. As the official legal entity and Employer of Record, the Fiscal Sponsor organization can get sued if something terrible happens at your program or with your staff. Because of this liability, Fiscal Sponsors carefully consider the risk factors of the work that you want to do and typically reserve the authority to make executive decisions that affect your program if anything about your work puts the Fiscal Sponsor's 501c3 status at risk or could put them in any legally risky situation.

The Fiscal Sponsor you choose should list the services they will provide and the fees they will charge you in the agreement you sign. The below image and the following section give you a sense of the types of services that a Fiscal Sponsor may offer.

Nonprofit Entity Status Layer

State Incorporation

- Every Fiscal Sponsor will provide you with an incorporated and registered nonprofit corporation at the state level; this is an annual filing.

- Your Fiscal Sponsor will have to register to solicit in every State you want to fundraise and operate in

    - Ensure they can legally operate in the State you want to work in.

- The Fiscal Sponsor should provide you with a State Charitable Organization Certificate, which will let you avoid sales tax if your State has a sales tax.

Federal 501c3 tax-deductible status

- Your donor will be eligible for tax deductions for the money, services, and items they donate to you. It would help if you asked for an IRS Determination Letter that provides proof to your donors that you have tax-deductible status.

- If the Fiscal Sponsor does something wrong, they can lose this status.

990 Tax Return

- Your project will be included in the Fiscal Sponsor's annual tax return. When applying for grants and funders request one or more years of 990s, you can use the Fiscal Sponsor's 990s (even if your organization wasn't under the Fiscal Sponsor's umbrella in previous years).

- All 990s are public records and easily searchable.

- When considering a Fiscal Sponsor, look up their 990 (https://projects.propublica.org/nonprofits/) to understand their financials. On the 990, you can see how much money they manage and if they lost money or had a budget surplus in previous years.

- 990s also list any employees paid over $100K by the organization, so you can also see how much the senior leadership team earns.

Legal Compliance Layer

Board of Directors

- Because the Fiscal Sponsor is the legal entity for your organization, the Fiscal Sponsor's Board of Directors has legal and fiduciary oversight over your organization. You should ask the potential Fiscal Sponsor questions about their board, including board diversity, if you are allowed to contact them (they are often funders), and if there are any conflicts of interest between them and your work.

- You should develop your own Board of Advisors for your organization to support you and assist with strategic planning and fundraising. However, they will not have legal oversight.

Independent Audit

- Most nonprofits that manage a large amount of money are legally required to have an annual financial audit to review their accounting records and policies to flag any issues and ensure that their funds are well managed. Most Fiscal Sponsors are well above the minimum threshold to trigger an audit. Your project will be included in the Fiscal Sponsor's annual Audit, and when you are applying for grants and funders request one or more years of audited financial statements, you can use the Fiscal Sponsor's (even if your organization wasn't under the Fiscal Sponsor's umbrella in previous years).

- When considering a Fiscal Sponsor, you should ask them for their recent audits to see if the auditors raised any red flags. This will help you determine whether the Fiscal Sponsor you choose is financially stable and well-managed.

Insurance

- Your Sponsor should have the following insurance policies at a minimum and should be able to provide you with a copy of their Insurance Certification.

    - Directors and Officers Insurance

    - General Liability

    - Theft & Fraud Coverage

    - Professional Liability

    - Worker's Compensation (if you have employees)

- It is also very important to understand your program's or your liability if something goes wrong. If an insurance claim is triggered by you or your program's activity, for example, if someone gets hurt at your program or if someone files a lawsuit saying they were harassed or illegally fired, the Fiscal Sponsor may hold you personally or your program financially liable for the insurance deductible or other associated legal expenses. Some Fiscal Sponsors may have a very high insurance deductible (as high as $50,000), for which you could be on the hook for in these situations. This issue should be addressed in your Fiscal Sponsorship agreement, so be cautious and read the fine print!

Legal Signatures

- Since the Fiscal Sponsor is the official legal entity, only the Fiscal Sponsor's authorized signers (usually their top executives) are allowed to sign any legally binding agreement on your behalf; this includes things like:

    - Property Leases

- Grant Award Letters
- Service Contracts

Employer of Record

- As the sole legal entity, your Fiscal Sponsor will be the employer of record for you and any staff you have

- The Fiscal Sponsor, as Employer of Record, is liable for any Human Resources-related legal matters

- Make sure that you understand the employee benefits your Fiscal Sponsor provides, and what those benefits will cost your project, like the employer-side costs of health insurance, etc.

Back Office Layer

Financial Services

Ultimately, your Fiscal Sponsor is legally responsible for managing your money, including how your revenue and expenses are accounted for, and they are usually subject to an independent audit every year. All professional Fiscal Sponsors provide some level of financial management services, but the level and quality of those services vary from Fiscal Sponsor to Fiscal Sponsor.

Most Fiscal Sponsors do not have separate bank accounts for each project they manage, so your funds are mixed in with all the other fiscally sponsored organizations' funds at the bank. This means that the Fiscal Sponsor must have good systems to track your income and expenses, ensure that programs don't overspend, and provide accurate financial reporting, including monthly statements. It is always a good step to double-check and verify the financial statements they provide to you. Fiscal sponsors should also ensure that your funds are used solely to support your mission and that your money is spent on eligible expenses that comply with IRS and funder guidelines.

Knowing who will be doing this work for you is also important. Is one person assigned to your account? Is it a team? How much experience do they have in nonprofit accounting? Are they local or remote, and how much direct access to them do you have?

Minimum Financial Services to expect:

- Accept funds via check, ACH/wire, and online on your behalf

- Provide donation receipts to your donors for their taxes

- Provide monthly financial reporting to you

- Pay bills and invoices for your program's expenses

- Process reimbursements for you and your staff when you provide documentation of eligible expenses

- Sign service contracts and award letters

- Invoice your funders and provide funders with the required financial documentation

Additional Financial Services to ask about:

- Accepting Government Contracts. Some Fiscal Sponsors don't work with government funding or charge extra for this service. Government funding (whether from local, state, or federal sources) often comes with complexity and regulations that require extra work and expertise from the Fiscal Sponsor. If you think your organization may want to apply for government funding, ask a potential Fiscal Sponsor about this before signing up.

- Providing a line of credit. While some funders will give you all or a portion of your grant funding upfront, others use a reimbursement model. Under a reimbursement model, you must pay upfront for your expenses and then invoice the Funder (often with receipts and other documentation). If you are invoicing the Funder monthly (or even less frequently for some funders) and then waiting for them to reimburse you, this can lead to cash flow issues for your organization, where you don't have access to enough money to pay your bills while you wait for reimbursement. Some Fiscal Sponsors will give you access to a line of credit, which means you can use the credit line if you don't have cash on hand to cover these up-front costs. This can be a huge help, so be sure to ask about this if you anticipate needing it (often, government funders use this model, but some other funders do as well). [You may want to add something about the FS charging a fee when offering use of the line of credit.]

- Cash Advances or Purchase Cards

- Accept Stock Donations or Crypto-Currency

- Help with developing budgets for grant proposals.

- Long-term financial planning or budgeting

Operational Services

These operational services may or may not be provided to you as part of your fiscal sponsorship agreement, or may be an additional expense for your Project, but make sure you ask.

- Office and or Meeting Space

- Mailbox/Mailing Address

- Mailing/Shipping Services

- Photocopying Services

- Purchasing Services

- IT Services

- Legal Services

- Contract Management

- Grant Management

HR Services

These HR services may or may not be provided to you as part of your fiscal sponsorship agreement, or may be an additional expense for your Project, but make sure you ask.

- Recruiting
- Job Posting
- Interview Support
- Hiring and Terminations
- Compensation Package support
- Workers Comp Insurance
- Payroll services
- Benefits Package
    - Health, Vision, and Dental Insurance
    - 401k / 403b Retirement plans
        - Employee match
    - Life Insurance

Partnership Services

- Coaching and Consulting Support
- Professional Development
- Fiscal Sponsor Orientations and Systems Training
- Resource Sharing

- Grant Databases
- Grant Writing Support
- Online Fundraising Platforms
- Networking
- Funder Introductions

The Cost of Fiscal Sponsorship

Each Fiscal Sponsor may charge different fees and may provide different levels and types of service. Still, as a general rule, you can expect to pay between 5% and 15% of the money you raise for Fiscal Sponsorship. Some Fiscal Sponsors will charge more if you receive government funding because it is more complicated to manage than most other funding. Some Fiscal Sponsors have minimum monthly fees, startup fees, or charges for other extra items. It's important to get a full list of fees and services from a potential Fiscal Sponsor before making your decision so that there are no surprises.

Part Two: Why Fiscal Sponsorship

Is Fiscal Sponsorship Right for Your Vision?

Now that I have explained Fiscal Sponsorship, the first critical decision you have to make is whether Fiscal Sponsorship is right for you. Being in a Fiscal Sponsorship relationship is a true partnership, where you trust your partner to manage your money for you and keep you in compliance with all of the regulations and laws that apply to 501c3 organizations. It can sometimes feel like a parent/child relationship more than an equal partnership, but the only alternative to Fiscal Sponsorship is getting your own 501c3.

It's not what this book is about, but for quick reference, here is what it takes to get your own 501c3:

If you want to get your 501c3, follow the steps below. State and federal fees can add up to over $800, and if you want to hire a lawyer or use an online service, you can add thousands of dollars to complete the items below. Then, depending on your programming, you will have to get your insurance, which will be another few thousand dollars.

It will usually take 4-8 months for the IRS to review and approve or deny your application.

Acquire State Incorporation

- Register your nonprofit's name in your State.

- Decide where to incorporate your nonprofit.

- Choose the board of directors.

- Create and sign your nonprofit corporation's articles of incorporation.

- File your nonprofit corporation's articles of incorporation with your State's secretary and pay any related fees.

Acquire Federal 501c3 Status.

- Write your nonprofit corporation's bylaws.

- Apply for 501(c)(3) tax-exempt status. You may receive a tax exemption from the local, State, and federal governments.

    - Form 1023 Checklist

    - Form 2848, Power of Attorney and Declaration of Representative (if filing)

    - Form 8821, Information Authorization (if filing)

    - Expedite request (if requesting)

    - Application (Form 1023 and Schedules A through H, as required)

    - Articles of organization

    - Amendments to articles of organization in chronological order

    - Bylaws or other rules of operation and amendments

    - Documentation of nondiscriminatory policy for schools, as required by Schedule B

    - Form 5768, Election/Revocation of Election by an Eligible Section 501(c)(3) Organization To Make

    - Expenditures To Influence Legislation (if filing)

    - All other attachments, including explanations, financial data, and printed materials or publications. Label each page with name and EIN.

- Open a separate bank account for your nonprofit corporation.

- Get Directors and Officers and General Liability Insurance

Then, you will have to file your 990 Tax return every year and keep up your state registration. Based on your revenue, the State you are registered in will ask you to pay for a full third-party audit, which can cost thousands of dollars. If you did not manage your funds correctly, the auditors will add those notes to your audit filing, which will be seen by your funders and is considered a public document.

There is also the 1023EZ form, which is much faster and cheaper to use, but you have to commit to staying under $50,000/year in revenue for the first three years of operations to maintain your status.

This is why I say: Skip The C3

Who uses Fiscal Sponsorship and Why

There are many benefits to being fiscally sponsored, especially if running your organization is not a full-time job or paperwork is not your strong suit. You get the benefits of plugging into an existing infrastructure and not having to "reinvent the wheel" and build up your organizational structure from scratch. You also get to buy into the Fiscal Sponsor's economies of scale, which means you are getting better services at a much lower cost than you could buy as a small independent 501c3; once your organization grows to be a multi-million-dollar budget, it may be cheaper for you to become independent, depending on your org's complexity and funders. Yet there are many fiscally sponsored organizations that have budgets in the tens of millions. These mega-projects may choose to stay fiscally sponsored for several strategic reasons. Using a Fiscal Sponsor, you are essentially outsourcing your organization's administration and financial management needs so you can focus on your mission and not worry about "generally accepted accounting principles" and IRS regulations.

Fiscal Sponsorship works for all types of nonprofit activity, for example:

Short-term or temporary projects

If you want to do a one-day event or something that only takes a few weeks or months a year, like Unity Week, a summer camp, or 5k Race, you don't need a 501c3 that costs money to run year-round.

Startup organizations and pilot programs

Fiscal Sponsors are often seen as "nonprofit incubators," because it is a lot easier to launch and manage a new organization with the established professional support of a Fiscal Sponsor, since they have access to a knowledge base and a team of experts. When a group wants to move quickly and not wait to file paperwork with your state and federal governments, it could take a year for the IRS to provide you with your 501c3 status. Fiscal Sponsorship can serve as a launching ground for pilot programs or proof-of-concept, allowing you to test your idea to see if you can attract funding and run an effective program without requiring you to invest in developing an administrative infrastructure. Launching your organization under the oversight of a Fiscal Sponsor can also lend credibility to your program. It can help reassure funders that the funding will be managed properly if they invest in your organization. As your organization grows, you can choose to remain with your Fiscal Sponsor or separate and branch off independently.

One of the great things about having a startup under a Fiscal Sponsor is that many funders will ask for three years of financial reports and tax returns; this demand automatically disqualifies startups for a large percentage of funding. Under a Fiscal Sponsor, you submit their financial reports and tax returns. You can also look like a much bigger organization on paper. For example, when funders say they only support organizations with budgets over one million dollars, you can submit your Fiscal Sponsors' budgets and financial reports. If the Funder will only fund smaller budgeted organs, you can tell them that you are fiscally sponsored and share your program's budget to show that you qualify for the funding. This provides the Funder with security that their funds will be properly managed, but you will still have to convince the Funder that your program is worth funding regardless of your financial stability.

For-profits that want to do charitable activities:

Suppose you have a for-profit company but want to do nonprofit work or go after nonprofit money. In that case, it's good to work with a Fiscal Sponsor who can service your needs as you need them and provide enough firewall compliance so that your 501c3 and your nonprofit don't get in trouble when it comes to money management, double dipping, and board maleficence. Also, when for-profits start and primarily fund their nonprofit, they may fail the IRS's Public Support Test, which could lead to the <u>loss of charitable deductibility for larger donors, again retroactively. Even worse, the organization cannot convert back to a public charity for at least five forward years.</u> By using a Professional Fiscal Sponsor you and the Sponsor will never face or fail the IRS's Public Support Test.

Established organizations:

Even if you have an established nonprofit that has been around for a few years or decades, there may be a reason to join a Fiscal Sponsor. For example, if you lose a major grant or contract or the economy falters and find yourself in a budget crunch, a Fiscal Sponsor can provide similar services for less money without losing quality. If your organization is in distress, say a sudden leadership change or issues of fiscal mismanagement are causing harm at the administrative level, your funders may even strongly encourage or demand you find a Fiscal Sponsor to stabilize the organization. For example, a city-funded homeless shelter is too big and important to fail. The City as Funder may not be happy with the shelter's administrators even when the programming is solid. Instead of shutting it down and forcing people back into the streets, the Funder will demand the organization go under a Fiscal Sponsor for a few years or longer until it can get management capacity strong enough to become independent again if it desires to.

Even without a crisis, it may make financial sense for an existing organization to enter into a Fiscal Sponsorship arrangement, depending on different factors such as the organization's size, cash flow needs, and compliance burden. Organizations that are volunteer-led or who have only part-time staff may be particularly well suited to a Fiscal Sponsorship arrangement. Even mid-sized organizations with a full-time staff may find it beneficial. Most nonprofit founders start an organization because they are passionate about doing good work in their communities, only to find themselves bogged down in paperwork, spreadsheets, and compliance questions. Joining a Fiscal Sponsor frees up your time and energy to focus on your mission and leave the legalese to someone else.

Foundations and Government Agencies:

Foundations and public agencies also often use Fiscal Sponsors if they want to launch new initiatives or need to move quickly on an opportunity and want to do something where there may not be an appropriate existing organization available; in that instance, they may turn to a Fiscal Sponsor that can quickly support and set up an organization on its infrastructure.

Myths of Fiscal Sponsorship

Because this is not a well-known model of nonprofit work, there are a lot of myths about Fiscal Sponsorship.

I will lose control of my organization.

A Fiscal Sponsor's job is to ensure that you comply with all the rules and laws of the land that cover your fundraising and program activity. Including the restrictions, rules, and regulations tied to the money you raise. Most Fiscal Sponsors do not want to micromanage your program. Their priority is not monitoring your day-to-day activities, it's monitoring the money. You can run your program as you see fit as long as you are not breaking any rules or laws. For example, you will have to work with your Sponsor's HR team to properly hire and fire someone because the Sponsor is the legal entity, the employer of record, and they bear the responsibility and liability of the people you hire and fire. They will ensure you do it so that there are no legal ramifications, which is what we all should want.

This is just for startups.

Fiscal Sponsorship is not always an accelerator or incubator of nonprofits. Many fiscally sponsored organizations have been that way for decades and even generations. Fiscal Sponsor also rarely provide the mentorship and support that a startup accelerator or incubator are designed to provide.

It's expensive.

Normally, when you engage a Fiscal Sponsor and it wants 10 or 15% of every dollar you raise, that one big number can feel like a lot. But the Fiscal Sponsor services you receive cover many, many budget lines in your budget and in general, Fiscal Sponsorship is usually cheaper than acquiring these services on your own. What you're getting from a Fiscal Sponsor is economies of scale that you can't achieve on your own. After all, a $30 million organization usually gets better pricing on everything from computers to cell phones to paper to insurance rates to HR benefits – that as an independent agency, even a million-dollar one, isn't able to qualify for. Most agencies who use Fiscal Sponsors find that in the end, it saves them money.

Risks of Fiscal Sponsorship

The primary risk of Fiscal Sponsorship is that the Fiscal Sponsor is a legal entity that you do not have any control over. Still, they are handling your money, programming, and staff, which is why it is incredibly important to have a contract between you and the Sponsor that lays out how money, liability, intellectual property, and program management is managed and what your and their responsibilities are. It's also important to have clear language on how the arrangement can be terminated.

The risk goes two ways - the Sponsor is legally liable for your organization's actions, and if something goes wrong, it is *they that* get sued, not you; because of this shared risk, the Fiscal Sponsor will have controls in place to reduce any risk you could put them in.

Having a strong contract between you and the Sponsor will greatly reduce the risks of being under Fiscal Sponsorship. But there is another major, although extremely rare, risk with being fiscally sponsored: the Sponsor gets into a poor financial position and collapses with your money. This has only happened a handful of times over the last thirty years.

In 2021, in Baltimore, Maryland, a well-established Fiscal Sponsor, Strong City Baltimore, grew too big too fast and failed to manage the funds in their trust properly. Sponsees needed access to their funds, leadership quit, the City's Inspector General got involved, and it was a mess.

"Due to Strong City's mismanagement of project finances, programs that provide vital services to the community were forced to shut their doors. Hundreds of people's livelihoods were compromised, forcing them to turn to unemployment and causing them to lose their medical benefits and job security." [1]

In 2012, a large-scale Fiscal Sponsor based in California, the International Humanities Center, imploded suddenly and mysteriously with all of their client's money.

"IHC was a Fiscal Sponsor for over two hundred groups (its list of projects numbered as many as three hundred, by some reports), largely politically or culturally progressive activist organizations, all of which were blindsided by the news that it had gone out of business. Most disturbing of all was news that the funding that IHC held and managed for these groups had largely evaporated." [2]

It's largely because of these incidents that I wrote this book: to inform you and ensure you are a fully educated consumer regarding Fiscal Sponsorship. When Fiscal Sponsorship is done right, it can be mutually beneficial for all concerned; but it's incumbent upon you to understand the type of relationship you are getting into and the consequences of it.

Part Three: Entering into a Fiscal Sponsorship Arrangement

What to ask when shopping for a Fiscal Sponsor

Remember, every Fiscal Sponsor is unique, and since there are no laws, regulations, or certifying agencies governing Fiscal Sponsors, it is very important to interview your Fiscal Sponsor as much as they are interviewing you.

Here is a checklist of questions that your Fiscal Sponsor should be able to answer with ease:

- What is their specific scope of services?
- What are the specific and mandatory things you must commit to (meetings, training, etc.)?
- Is the Fiscal Sponsor registered to operate, solicit, and handle payroll in the State or States that you want to operate in?
- Ask for their last independent Audit so you can review it for any Audit letters or findings (red flags)
- Ask for their Board list - is it diverse, who is on it, and does the Board have to approve project applications? Are there interactions between the Board and the Project?
- Ask what all their fees are, startup costs, budget minimums, etc.
- What kind of insurance do they have?
    - They should at least have $1M of coverage that should include:
        - Directors and Officers
        - General Liability

- Event
- Theft
- Honesty/Fraud

- Who is assigned as my contact? You should have access to a combination of:
    - An Accountant or fiscal manager
    - An HR Manager, if you have or will have employees
    - A Partnership Manager/Liaison who would be your primary contact
- What are the HR Benefits for Employees?
- Do I need an Advisory Board, and at what size and how often do they need to meet?
- What is the minimum account balance I can have in my accounts?
- What if I am inactive for a while?
- How do you manage Intellectual Property?
- Am I Personally Liable for anything that happens?
- How do you handle lobbying and political activity?
- How is the money managed?
- What systems do I have to learn or use with you?
- How do checks get cut, and how often? Weekly, Monthly?
- How do people get paid?
- Do they provide fundraising support?
- Do they provide a line of credit for grants that require reimbursement?

- Do they issue credit cards?
- How do they handle these types of transactions?
    - Online Giving
    - Stock Donations
    - Crypto Donations
    - Cash Donations
    - In-kind donations
    - Property donations
    - Sales
    - Earned revenue
- Get Referrals
- Google them

Fiscal Sponsorship Contract Negotiation

Once you are ready to sign a Fiscal Sponsorship agreement, you should be prepared to review it critically; if you have a lawyer available, it is best to have them review it. These agreements vary from Fiscal Sponsor to Fiscal Sponsor, but the following items should be addressed in the agreement and written in a way that is agreeable to you:

1. **Term** - How long is the agreement for? Does it auto-renew?

2. **Personal Liability** - as a signor of the agreement, is there any language that would make you personally liable for any financial issues that arise from being fiscally sponsored? Such liabilities may include if your organization is in debt or owes money to the Fiscal Sponsor or if a claim against your organization triggers an insurance claim.

3. **Exiting** - Does the agreement clearly outline how and when you can leave the Fiscal Sponsor

4. **Fees** - all fees should be listed and explained.

5. **Fund Management** - how are your funds managed, and who has access to them?

6. **Intellectual property** - how do they hold your intellectual property, and how do they release it to you when you leave?

7. **Scope of Services** - does the agreement lay out the services they will provide, what parts of nonprofit operations they will be responsible for, and what parts you will be responsible for

See the index for annotated Fiscal Sponsorship agreements.

What the Fiscal Sponsor is going to ask for

Fundamentally, the point of a Fiscal Sponsor is to manage the money you raise and provide your donors with a tax deduction. While mission fit is also a core issue for the Fiscal Sponsor, most Fiscal Sponsors have a mission fit that can fit a lot; there has to be fundamental value alignment with their and your mission. As long as you are a mission fit and can raise enough money to meet their requirements, you are likely to be selected by a Fiscal Sponsor. They will still ask you to complete an application; many will also do an interview and, based on your organization's size and history, a deep dive into your history and operations. For example, there are common questions you will have to answer:

- Name / Mission Statement
- Programming Description
    - Real or planned
        - This should be very detailed
- Why is this organization unique?

- Website and social media
- Who are your partners?
- Where will you find your participants?
- Did you do a pilot? (Share any data from that if so)
- Why are you qualified to run it?
- Who is on your team
    - Founder(s)?
    - Advisory Board or Mentors
    - Staff Bios and Job Descriptions
        - These can be for existing jobs or anticipated ones
- Budget
    - Should include revenue and expenses, and should add up to a zero or a small surplus, ideally
    - Salaries should be in line with the local market
    - See the Sample in the index
- Fundraising plan to meet your Budget needs
    - Do you have donors lined up
    - Grants Identified
    - Earned Revenue Plans?

See samples of applications in the index.

What Fiscal Sponsors will say NO to 99% of the time.

There are times when a Fiscal Sponsor won't be able to accept your organization as its risk factor is too high and may put the Fiscal Sponsor's 501c3 in jeopardy or hurt the existing organizations. For example, a Fiscal Sponsor may reject a partnership with a startup that

- Discriminates in any way
- Is a church or religious institution
- International Money Transfers
    - Sending money overseas
    - Products are ok, but no currency
- Anything that is self-serving or looks like "washing the money through a nonprofit."
- Have high-risk activities like
    - Kids in Caves
    - Kids and Powertools
    - Kids and Contact Sports
- Government Grants – Many Fiscal Sponsors do not accept government funding for various reasons, including their complexity and their cash flow requirements.

This is not all of them, but you can see that Fiscal Sponsors are risk-averse because they have to manage hundreds of semi-autonomous organizations with different and sometimes the same Funder and one bad apple can spoil the bunch.

INDEX

List of Fiscal Sponsors

Source: https://fiscalsponsordirectory.org/ 12/5/23

\#

1st Note Music Foundation – Denver, CO
50CAN, Inc. – Washington, D.C.

A

The Abundance Foundation – Pittsboro, NC
Accessible Festivals – Stockton, NJ
Afram Global Organization Inc. – Bellflower, CA
African Voices Communications, Inc. – New York, NY
AfroPresencia – Brooklyn, NY
A God Send – Orange Park, FL
AIDS Connecticut (ACT) – Hartford, CT
AJ Muste Memorial Institute – New York, NY
Alliance for Global Justice – Tucson, AZ
Allied Arts Foundation – Seattle, WA
Alternative Newsweekly Foundation – Washington, D.C.
American Muslim Community Foundation – Fremont, CA
Angels for Angels – Seattle, WA
Another Choice, Another Chance – Sacramento, CA
Art of the Matter – San Francisco, CA
Artportunity Knocks – Atlanta, GA
Artrain – Ann Arbor, MI
Arts Alive! Inc. – Keene, NH
Arts & Business Council of Greater Nashville – Nashville, TN
Arts Services Inc. – Buffalo, NY
Association Building Community – Oakland, CA
Austin Creative Alliance – Austin, TX
Austin Film Society – Austin, TX

B

Baltimore Civic Fund – Baltimore, MD
BASICS – Milwaukee, WI
Bay Area Community Resources – San Rafael, CA

Bay Area Video Coalition – San Francisco, CA
BE Meditation Group – Los Angeles, CA
Bmore Empowered Inc. – Baltimore, MD
Berkeley Art Center – Berkeley, CA
Berkeley Partners for Parks – Berkeley, CA
Betty Jean Brown Foundation – Lafayette, CA
The Big Picture Film and Video Foundation – Atlanta, GA
Billings Community Foundation – Billings, MT
The Biodiversity Group – Tucson, AZ
Blue Earth Alliance – Seattle, WA
Boise Film Foundation – Boise, ID
Boston Dance Alliance – Boston, MA
Boulder County Arts Alliance – Boulder, CO
Broncos Kitchen Foundation – Kalamazoo, MI
Brooklyn Arts Council – Brooklyn, NY
Brown Girl Wellness, Inc. – Baltimore, MD
Buddhist Film Foundation, Inc. – Berkeley, CA

C

The Carla Rose Foundation, Inc. – Spartanburg, SC
CascadiaNow! – Seattle, WA
Center for Community Stewardship – Madison, WI
Center for Independent Documentary Inc. – Boston, MA
Center for Social Change – Miami, FL
Center for Transformative Action – Ithaca, NY
Center for Volunteer and Nonprofit Leadership – San Rafael, CA
CENTER Santa Fe – Santa Fe, NM
Chabot-Las Positas Community College District – Pleasanton, CA
The Chainges Fund, Inc. – Atlanta, GA
Chalice Oak Foundation – Rancho Palos Verdes, CA
Chappy & Friends – Chicago, IL
Charitable Ventures – Santa Ana, CA
Charity Music, Inc – Sterling Heights, MI
Chicago Filmmakers – Chicago, IL
Children's Network of Solano County – Fairfield, CA
City Lore – New York, NY
Clearwater Resource Conservation and Development Council, Inc. – Moscow, ID
Cloud Forest Institute – Ukiah, CA
Colorado Nonprofit Development Center – Denver, CO

Color My Outdoors – Asheville, NC
Columbia Basin Foundation – Ephrata, WA
Community2gether Inc. – Warwick, NY
Community Capital Fund – Kansas City, MO
Community Coordinated Child Care (4-C) – Madison, WI
Community Foundation for the National Capital Region – Washington, D.C.
Community Foundation of Brazoria County – Angleton, TX
Community Initiatives – Oakland, CA
Community LIFT – Memphis, TN
Community Partners – Los Angeles, CA
Community Shares Tennessee – Knoxville, TN
Conscious Goodness – Santa Monica, CA
CORE Foundation Inc. – Reston, VA
Corry Community Development Corporation – Corry, PA
CORE Community Organized Relief Effort – Los Angeles, CA
Create Wisconsin – Madison, WI
Creative Many Michigan – Detroit, MI
Creative Visions – Malibu, CA
CultureTrust Greater Philadelphia – Philadelphia, PA

D

Dalit Solidarity – San Diego, CA
Dance Films Association – Brooklyn, NY
Dance Resource Center – Los Angeles, CA
Dancers' Group – San Francisco, CA
DAS Foundation Inc. – Phoenix, AZ
Daylight Community Arts Foundation – Bronx, NY
Del Mar Foundation – Del Mar, CA
Del Valle Community Coalition Non-Profit – Austin, TX
Denver Film – Denver, CO
Docs In Progress – Silver Spring, MD
Documentary Educational Resources – Watertown, MA

E

Earth Island Institute – Berkeley, CA
East Bay Asian Local Development Corporation – Oakland, CA
Ecologistics Inc. – Los Osos, CA
Education Consortium of Central Los Angeles – Los Angeles, CA

Educational Media Foundation, Inc. – Richmond Hill, GA
Edward Charles Foundation – Beverly Hills, CA
Empower Me – Roebuck, SC
Empowerment Works – Oakland, CA
Evergreen Social Impact – Bothell, WA
EveryLibrary Institute NFP – Berwyn, IL

F

Faith Based Nonprofit Resource Center – Elkton, MD
The Federated Charities Corporation of Frederick – Frederick, MD
Federation of Neighborhood Centers – Philadelphia, PA
Fideicomiso de Conservación de Puerto Rico – San Juan, Puerto Rico
The Field – New York, NY
The Film Collaborative – Los Angeles, CA
Film Independent – Los Angeles, CA
FilmNorth – St. Paul MN
Filmmakers Collaborative, Inc. – Waltham, MA
Financial Services Coalition — Puget Sound Charitable Foundation – Seattle, WA
Fiscal Sponsorship Allies Inc. – Indianapolis, IN
FJC – New York, NY
The Foraker Group – Anchorage, AK
Force for Good Community Development Corporation – Gary, In
Foundation for California Community Colleges – Sacramento, CA
Foundation for Independent Artists, Inc. (FIA) – New York, NY
Foundation for Louisiana – Baton Rouge, LA
Foundation For Montana History – Helena, MT
Foundation for the Mid South – Jackson, MS
Foundation for National Progress – San Francisco, CA
Fractured Atlas – New York, NY
Fraternal Order of Eagles #3142 – Chula Vista, CA
Fresh Arts – Houston, TX
Friends of the Future – Kamuela, HI
From the Heart Productions – Oxnard, CA
Fulcrum Arts – Pasadena, CA
Full Spectrum Features NFP – Chicago, IL
Fundación Comunitaria de Puerto Rico – San Juan, Puerto Rico
Fund for Constitutional Government – Washington, D.C.

The FUSION Foundation – Scottsdale, AZ
Fusion Partnerships, Inc. – Baltimore, MD

G

Give2Asia – San Francisco, CA
Givsum Foundation – Newport Beach, CA
The Giving Back Fund – Los Angeles, CA
Global Center – New York, NY
Global Fund for Women – San Francisco, CA
Global Health Review – Venice, CA
Global Horizons Inc. – Burnsville, MN
Global Impact – Alexandria, VA
Global Peace Media – Ramsey, NJ
GOH Productions – New York, NY
Good Causes, Inc. – Albany, NY
Goodcity N.F.P. – Chicago, IL
Goodnation Foundation – New York, NY
The Good Rural – San Francisco, CA
The Gotham Center for New York City History – New York, NY
The Gotham Film & Media Institute – New York, NY
Grant Assistance Services Inc. – Galliano, LA
Green Umbrella – Cincinnati, OH

H

The Hack Foundation – West Hollywood, CA
Hacker Fund – Santa Monica, CA
HASER, Inc. – San Juan, Puerto Rico
Heaven's Door Cancer Foundation – San Francisco, CA
The Hektoen Institute for Medical Research – Chicago, IL
Heluna Health – City of Industry, CA
Hired to Home, Inc. – New York, NY
Houston Cinema Arts Society – Houston, TX
Hudson County Latino Foundation – Jersey City, N.J.
Humanitarian Social Innovations – Bethlehem, PA

I

Image Essays – Houston, TX
Impact Philanthropy Group – Long Beach, CA
Independent Arts and Media – San Francisco, CA

Independent Pictures – Cleveland, OH
Ink People Inc. – Eureka, CA
Inquiring Systems, Inc. – Sonoma , CA
Inside and Out Project – Casa Grande, AZ
Institute for Education, Research, and Scholarships – Los Angeles, CA
Institute for Nonprofit News – Los Angeles, CA
InterMusic SF – San Francisco, CA
The International Association of Blacks in Dance, Inc. – Silver Spring, MD
International Documentary Association – Los Angeles, CA
International Friendship Through the Performing Arts – Eagan, MN
International Information Policy Foundation, Inc. – New York, NY
The Interreligious Foundation for Community Organization – New York, NY
Intersection for the Arts – San Francisco, CA
ioby – Brooklyn, NY

J

Jewish Creativity International – New York, NY
Jumpstart Labs – Santa Monica, CA

K

Kidz Success, Inc. – Sacramento, CA
KlezCalifornia – El Cerrito, CA

L

Ladies In Transit Holistic Community Development Corporation – Riverside, NJ
Land Conservation and Advocacy Trust, Inc. – Framingham, MA
The Learners Lab Foundation (TLLF) – Lanham, MD
Let's Bring Them Home – Bentonville, AR
Local Color – San Jose, CA
Local Media Foundation – Lake City, MI
Lokahi Pacific – Wailuku, HI
Los Altos Community Foundation – Los Altos, CA
Love Foundation – Chicago, IL

M

Marcus Foster Education Institute – Oakland, CA
MarinLink – San Rafael, CA
The Marion Institute – Marion, MA
Mayan Spring Inc.– Queens, NY
Maysles Documentary Center – Harlem, NY 10027
Media Alliance – San Francisco, CA
Media Arts Center San Diego – San Diego, CA
Midwest Artist Project Services (MAPS) – St. Louis, MO
Milwaukee, Film – Milwaukee, WI
Ministry Movement – Pensacola, FL
Mission Earth – Framingham, MA
Mission Edge – San Diego, CA
Mockingbird Incubator – Los Angeles, CA
Multicultural Self-Esteem Academy – Houston, TX
Multiplier – Oakland, CA

N

National Center for Jewish Film – Waltham, MA
National Center for Reason and Justice – Roxbury, MA
National Network of Public Health Institutes – New Orleans, LA
National Performance Network – New Orleans, LA
NEO Philanthropy – New York, NY
Netroots Foundation – San Francisco, CA
Nevada County Arts Council — Nevada City, CA
New Horizons Foundation Inc. – Colorado Springs, CO
New Mexico Community Foundation – Santa Fe, NM
New Mexico Dance Coalition – Santa Fe, NM
New Mexico Film Foundation – Santa Fe, NM
New Mexico Spotlight Foundation – Albuquerque, NM
New Sun Rising – Pittsburgh, PA
New York Foundation for the Arts – Brooklyn, NY
New York Live Arts – New York, NY
New York Women in Film & Television – New York, NY
Non Profit Accounting Service – Columbia, CA
Nonprofit Center of the Berkshires, Inc. – Great Barrington, MA
Nonprofit Enterprise at Work, Inc. – Ann Arbor, MI
Nonprofit Hub Foundation – Lincoln, NE
NOPI – Nonprofit Incubator – Norwood, MA
North Dakota Community Foundation – Bismarck, ND
North Kohala Community Resource Center – Hawaii, HI

North Woodward Community Foundation – Troy, MI
Northwest Alliance for Alternative Media and Education – Portland, OR
Northwest Film Forum – Seattle, WA
NotYetPro – Washington, D.C.

O

Oakland Parks and Recreation Foundation – Oakland, CA
Oakland Public Education Fund – Oakland, CA
Omprakash – Seattle, WA
On Da Verg – Ft. Worth, TX
On It Foundation – Miami, FL
OneOC – Santa Ana, CA
OOPS MN – Lakeville, MN
Open Collective Foundation – Walnut, CA
Open Media Foundation – Denver, CO
Open Space Institute Inc. – New York, NY
Oregon Wildlife Foundation – Portland, OR
Ozcat Entertainment – Vallejo, CA

P

Pacifica's Environmental Family – Pacifica, CA
Palms for Life Fund – New York, NY
PAM CUT – Portland, OR
Pan Left Productions – Tucson, AZ
Panorama Global – Seattle, WA
Paramount Personalized Learning, Inc. – Grand Prairie, TX
Partners of Parks – Long Beach, CA
Peace Development Fund – San Francisco, CA
Peace Development Fund – Amherst, MA
Pecan Street Inc. – Austin, TX
Pensacola Community Action Network, Inc. – Pensacola, Fla.
People In Partnership – Charleston, SC
Petya I. Edwards Foundation – Dallas, TX
Pittsburgh Filmmakers/Pittsburgh Center for the Arts – Pittsburgh, PA
Players Philanthropy Fund – Towson, MD
Pledges, Inc. – San Francisco, CA
POISE Foundation – Pittsburgh, PA

Power Shift Network – Washington, D.C.
Praxis Project – Oakland, CA
Preservation Alliance of Minnesota – St. Paul, MN
Progressives Educating New Yorkers, Inc. – New York, NY
Propel Nonprofits – Minneapolis, MN
Provincetown Community Compact – Provincetown, MA
Public Health Institute – Oakland, CA
Public Health Institute of Metropolitan Chicago – Chicago, IL
Public Health Solutions – New York, NY
Public Media Inc. – New York, NY

R

RVC Seattle – Seattle, WA
The Redford Center – San Francisco, CA
Reel Hope – Atlanta, GA
Resilience Partners NFP – Chicago, IL
Resources for Human Development – Philadelphia, PA
Rethink Charity – Mineral, VA
Rio Grande Community Development Corporation – Albuquerque, NM
Road to Artdom Foundation, Inc. – Los Angeles, CA
Rockefeller Philanthropy Advisors – New York, NY
Rose Foundation for Communities and the Environment – Oakland, CA
Russian Riverkeeper – Healdsburg, CA

S

San Francisco Beautiful – San Francisco, CA
San Francisco Early Music Society – Berkeley, CA
San Francisco Parks Alliance – San Francisco, CA
San Francisco Public Health Foundation – San Francisco, CA
San Francisco Study Center – San Francisco, CA
San Juan Resource Conservation & Development Council – Durango, CO
Santa Barbara Dance Alliance – Santa Barbara, CA
Sarah Webster Fabio Center for Social Justice – Richmond, CA
Satellite Collective ORBIT – Rockaway Park, NY
Schools without Borders – Toronto, ON, Canada
Seattle Parks Foundation – Seattle, WA

Service After Service – Alpharetta, GA
Service Dogs of Florida, Inc. – Winter Garden, FL
SE Uplift Neighborhood Coalition – Portland, OR
Seventh Generation Fund for Indian Development – Arcata, CA
Shunpike – Seattle, WA
Side Project Inc. – West Palm Beach, FL
Side Project Inc. – Pittsburgh, PA
Silent Hall of Fame – Moraga, CA
SIMA Studios – West Hollywood, CA
Siskiyou County Arts Council – Mount Shasta, CA
Social & Environmental Entrepreneurs – Calabasas, CA
Social Impact Fund – Los Angeles, CA
SocialGood – Oakland, CA
SOMArts – San Francisco, CA
Southern Conservation Partners, Inc. – Raleigh, NC
Southern Documentary Fund – Durham, NC
Southern Illinois Community Foundation – Marion, IL
Southern Vision Alliance – Durham, NC
Southwest Research and Information Center – Albuquerque, NM
Southwestern Colorado Area Health Education Center – Durango, CO
Springboard for the Arts – St. Paul, MN
Streams in the Desert Foundation, Inc. dba High Desert Community Foundation – Apple Valley, CA
Streams of Dreams, Inc. – Douglasville, GA
Sustainable Seattle – Seattle, WA
Sweet Home Community Foundation – Sweet Home, OR

T

TCF The Community's Foundation – Springfield, PA
Technical Assistance Partnership of Arizona (TAPAZ) – Phoenix, AZ
The Grateful Film Fund – Santa Monica, CA
The Ocean Foundation – Washington, D.C.
The Reading Room CLE – Cleveland, OH
Theater Resources Unlimited – New York, New York
#TeenWritersProject – Dallas, TX
Third World Newsreel – New York, NY
Tides Center – San Francisco, CA
Tiny Seed Project Inc. – Greensboro Bend, VT
Tomorrow's Education Network, Inc. – Towaco, NJ

Trailhead Institute – Denver, CO
Transformative Culture Project – Roxbury, MA
Trees Foundation – Redway, CA
Triangle ArtWorks – Raleigh, NC
TriCounty Community Network – Pottstown, PA
Truckee Meadows Parks Foundation – Reno, NV
TSNE – Boston, MA
Twin Rivers Council for the Arts – Mankato, MN

U

UI Charitable Advisors – Provo, UT
Unique Projects Inc. – New York, NY
United Charitable – Falls Church, VA
United Way of Southwest Colorado – Durango, CO 81302
Urban Affairs Coalition – Philadelphia, PA
Urban Mediamakers – Norcross, GA
Use The News Foundation – San Francisco, CA
U.S.-Mexico Border Philanthropy Partnership – San Diego, CA
Utah Cold Case Coalition – Salt Lake City, UT

V

Veterans Awareness Transition Corporation – Beverly, NJ
Village Earth – Fort Collins, CO
Visions Made Viable – Irvine, CA
VOW Foundation – Oswego, NY

W

Washington Research Institute – Ukiah, CA
The Watershed Project – Richmond, CA
We Bloom Inc.– Indianapolis, IN
Wellness Works, Inc. – Anchorage, AK
West Contra Costa Public Education Fund – Richmond, CA
WHOmentorsdotcom Inc. – San Jose, CA
Women in Film & Video – Washington, D.C.
Women Make Movies – New York, NY

WoMN ACT® (Advocate, Collaborate, Transform) – St. Paul, MN
The Woods Hole Film Festival – Woods Hole, MA

Y

Youth Leadership Incubator dba Hack+ – Fremont, CA
YWCA of Greater Portland – Portland, OR

CANADA

Schools without Borders – Toronto, ON, Canada

Sample Applications

The names of the Fiscal Sponsors have been removed from these applications, use these as a reference.

The Community Foundation ███████████

Fiscal Sponsor Application

Fiscal Sponsor - a tax-exempt charitable or social welfare group operating under a 501(c)(3) that has an arrangement with small community-based groups (SCBG) that **ARE NOT** registered NPOs

FISCAL SPONSOR/CONTACT INFORMATION

1. **Name of Fiscal Sponsor:**

2. **Do you have a Unique Entity Identifier UEI** (number issued by sam.gov):

    a) **Yes: Enter Here**

    b) **Pending: upload supporting document**

    b) **No: Explain**

3. **CEO/Executive Director/Signing Authority name**
Title:

Mailing Address :

City:

State:

Zip Code:

Phone Number:

Email Address:

☐ Check Here if Responsible Administrator is the same as above

4. **Responsible Administrator name (will receive all communications for the application):**
Title:

Mailing Address:

City:

State:

Zip Code:

Phone Number:

Email Address:

5. Will you perform ALL of the following functions on behalf of the small community-based groups:
   a) Receive grants, contributions, and other money on behalf of each of the small community-based groups

   b) Ensure that the money of each small community-based group is spent on the intended charitable purposes of the group

   c) Determine how and when the money of each small community-based group is spent

   d) Supervise each small community-based group's finances

   e) Ensure that each small community-based group's money is used in a manner that furthers the Fiscal Sponsor's own charitable work and

   f) Provide financial and project guidance to each small community-based group;

☐ Yes ☐ No

6. Can you perform these functions specified for an administrative fee that does not exceed ten percent (10%) of the total amount of any grant, contribution, or other money that the small community-based groups received with the assistance of the Fiscal Sponsor.
☐ Yes ☐ No

7. Insurance Requirement Acknowledgement:
As the Fiscal Sponsor I understand that if awarded, the following levels and certificates of insurance must be obtained to receive grant funds.
☐ Yes ☐ No

General Liability:

Each occurrence - $500,000 General Aggregate - $500,000

Products and completed operations aggregate - $500,000 Fire - $50,000

Automobile Liability:
Each occurrence $500,000

Cyber/Network Security and Privacy Liability:

Each occurrence - $500,000 General Aggregate - $1,000,000

Crime Insurance:
Each occurrence - $500,000 General Aggregate - $500,000

If No, please explain here:
_____

8. Is your organization in good standing with the Colorado Secretary of State?
☐ Yes ☐ No

Upload Proof of good standing status
Provide a Certificate of good standing with the State of ▇▇▇▇▇▇, Secretary of State Office. This document can be obtained at https://www.sos.state.▇▇.us/pubs/business/businessHome.html. Under "Services," click "Certificate of good standing."

9. If your organization is awarded funds, you will be required to submit backup documentation on all expenditures on a quarterly basis. Is this something your organization is able to do?
☐ Yes ☐ No Explain:
_____

B. SMALL COMMUNITY BASED GROUP ELIGIBILITY

The following information must be completed and submitted for each SCBG you are representing.

Name of the group:

1. What is the group's operating budget for the current fiscal year:

    a) Upload the group's operating budget for the current fiscal year:

2. Where is the main office of the group located (city and county)?

    What counties does the group serve?
(check list)

3. What is the group's mission?

4. Which of the following services does the group provide? (select all that apply)
☐ Health Equity   ☐ Workforce Development   ☐ Community Economic Development   ☐ Housing

☐ Food Justice   ☐ Education Support   ☐ Early Childhood Care

☐ **Other community identified need**
_____

Describe how the group provides services in the areas listed above? (500 word limit) Is there another group to add to this application?
☐ Yes ☐ No

C. COVID-19 IMPACT
Select and provide supporting documentation on how EACH group was impacted or disproportionately impacted by the COVID-19 Public Health Emergency

Supporting documentation can include, but is not limited to: Year over year budgets, board meeting minutes indicating discussion or vote, notes from board finance or other committee meetings, email documentation, signed letter from board chair documenting specific situation.

1. ☐ The group was disproportionately impacted by the COVID-19 Public Health Emergency
    a. Supporting Documentation:
    Note: *To qualify for the disproportionately impacted criteria the group must provide services in a qualified census tract, as defined by the United States treasury as any census tract that is designated by the secretary of housing and urban development and, for the most recent year for which census data are available on household income in such tract, either in which **50%** or more of the households have an income that is less than **60%** of the area median gross income for such year or that has a poverty rate of at least **25%**. Use this map to lookup qualified census tracts by address.*

2. ☐ The group's total operating budget has decreased during the COVID-19 public health emergency
    a. What % has the operating budget decreased?
    b. Supporting documentation:

3. ☐ The group had to lay off staff during the COVID-19 public health emergency
    a. What % of staff did they have to lay off during the COVID-19 public health emergency:
    b. Supporting documentation:

4. ☐ The group had to close for a period during the COVID-19 public health emergency
    a. What dates or date range was the group closed:
    b. Supporting documentation: _____

5. ☐ The group had to access its financial reserves to pay for operating costs during the COVID-19 public health emergency.
    a. What % of your financial reserves were accessed:
    b. Supporting documentation: _____

6. ☐ If none of the above apply, tell us how the group was impacted by the COVID-19 Public Health emergency. (500 word limit)

Upload one supporting document per group you are representing.

D. PROGRAM INFORMATION
Please answer the questions below as the collaborative of SCBG's.

This funding prioritizes support for communities who have been historically underrepresented, underserved,

or under-resourced in .

Indicate all the communities the groups serve (place an X in each applicable category):

LGBT	BIPOC	Women	Gender non-conforming	Disability/ neuro diversity	Low Income	Immigrant/ Refugee	Rural

1. Indicate below the whole of the groups staffs and boards representation of historically underrepresented, underserved, or under-resourced communities:

    Provide a number of staff and board that identify with the following categories:

	a) Board	b) Staff aff
LGBT		
BIPOC		
Women		

Gender Non-conforming		
Disability		
Low-Income		
Immigrant/Refugee		
Rural		
Total Unduplicated # represented		
Total Number in group		

c) Indicate which of the following communities the highest paid executive staff members identify with from the communities the group serves above (place an X in each applicable category):

LGBT	BIPOC	Women	Gender non-conforming	Disability/neurodiversity	Low Income	Immigrant/Refugee	Rural	N/A

2. Please answer the following questions in regard to the group's work that specifically focuses on historically underrepresented, underserved, or under-resourced communities.

    a) How do all of the groups ensure they're providing relevant programs? (500 word limit)

    b) How do all of the groups ensure that services are culturally responsive? (500 word limit)

    c) How do all of the groups ensure that the services they provide are effective? (500 word limit)

3. How do all of the groups take client and community feedback into consideration when deciding where to focus efforts? (500 word limit)

4. Do all of the groups connect the communities they serve with other state or federally funded programs?
☐ Yes ☐ No

E. PROJECT INFORMATION

Please answer the questions below as the collaborative of SCBG's.

1. Select the category of the project(s) (select all that apply):
These funds can be utilized for infrastructure and capacity building in the following categories. Please select all that apply to this request.

Note: requested amount cannot exceed 30% of the collective annual operating budget, max award amount is $100,000

    ☐ **Data Technology - data collection and/or technology infrastructure**

    ☐ **Professional Development - staff and board**

    ☐ **Communications**

    ☐ **Strategic planning and group's development for capacity building, fundraising, and other services**

    ☐ **Existing program expansion, development or evaluation**

    ☐ Other_____

2. Tell us about the project(s) and how each group will use the requested funds (500 word limit):

3. What is the timeline for the completion of the project(s)?

4. If this collective is awarded funds, they will be required to submit backup documentation on all expenses on a quarterly basis. Is this something the groups are able to do?
☐ Yes ☐ No Explain: _____

F. BUDGET

1. **Total amount of funds requested** (requested amount cannot exceed 30% of collective annual operating budget, max award amount - $100,000, Fiscal Sponsor administrative allowance = 10% of total award):

2. Total amount of administrative funds requested:

2. Budget narrative for funds requested:

Center for ▇▇▇▇ ▇▇▇▇ Leadership

Fiscal Sponsorship Application Questionnaire

Please complete all areas of the application (all fields are required for submission). For questions, contact ▇▇▇, Director of Finance and Operations: ▇▇▇▇▇▇.

Name of Project:

Date of request: **Name of Principal Contact:**

Title: **Telephone:**

Email:

Mailing Address:

1. What is the legal status of this project? (check one): Sole proprietorship
   **Unincorporated association California nonprofit corporation 501(c)(3) corporation
   California nonprofit corporation that has applied for 501(c)(3) status**

2. Purpose of the project (one sentence):

3. Current project assets (how much do you have now?): $

4. Anticipated annual budget: $

5. Anticipated source(s) of revenue:

6. Do you have an Advisory Committee? (check one below). Please list names and titles below if "yes."

    Yes

    No

7. Do you anticipate having employees, volunteers, and/or independent contractors? (check one):
**Yes No
If yes, how many of each?:**

Employees   **Volunteers**
                                           Independent contractors

8. Do you anticipate doing any lobbying? (check one): Yes
**No
If yes, please describe anticipated activities:**

9. Has the project created or acquired any significant intellectual property to date, or do you anticipate having any (e.g., website, program materials, electronic media, publications, graphics, photos, artwork, member or donor lists)?:
**Yes No
If yes, please describe:**

10. Do/would any of your anticipated project activities involve risk or require special insurance coverage?:
**Yes No
If yes, please describe:**

11. Do you anticipate any administrative difficulties for Center for Volunteer & Nonprofit Leadership in managing this project?:
**Yes No
If yes, please describe:**

12. Are you currently using another Fiscal Sponsor?: Yes
    No Name:

13. If you have a current Fiscal Sponsor, please describe their attitude toward this transfer:

14. Are you exploring other Fiscal Sponsors for this project?: Yes
    No Who?:

14. How did you find us?:

15. Project location/area of service by county (check all that apply): ☐

16. Field of interest (check all that apply): ☐Arts & Culture
    Education
    **Environment
    Health Human Services Public Affairs
    Other (please identify):**

17. Center for Volunteer & Nonprofit Leadership qualifier (check all that apply):

A project seeking incubation

- **Have you applied for a 501(c)(3) status?**
  Yes No

- **Do you anticipate applying within the next five years?**
  Yes No Maybe

A funder-instigated or multi-funder collaborative project

- **Is more than one foundation involved in launching this project?**
  Yes No

- **Is this project the result of a single funder's initiative?**
  Yes No

A project of limited duration

- Is this project a one-time special event? Yes **No**

- Do you anticipate this project being completed within the next two years? Yes **No**

- Do you anticipate this project being completed within the next five years Yes **No**

- Do you anticipate the project lasting ten years or more? Yes **No**

APPLICATION CHECKLIST

Have you:

Filled out all items on this questionnaire?

Attached a description of your project indicating the following?

- When it began
- Its size, scope, and aspirations
- Its nonprofit purpose
- The number of participants
- The target beneficiaries of your activity
- Attached an income-and-expense budget for this current year and past year, if available?
- Attached a list of your Advisory Committee

(minimum of three) with their contact information and brief biographies?

▓▓▓▓▓▓▓▓▓▓ ▓▓▓▓▓▓▓▓▓▓

Fiscal Sponsorship Application

Partner Your Project with ▓▓▓▓▓▓▓▓ ▓▓▓▓▓▓

We are so glad that you are interested in applying for Fiscal Sponsorship (https://▓▓.org/fiscal-sponsorship-nonprofit-incubation/) with ▓▓▓▓▓▓▓. Please fill out the application below to the best of your ability. You will be asked to upload specific information, and when you click "Send" a PDF copy of your application will be sent to your email for your records. We look forward to speaking personally about your project soon!

Name of Principal Contact *
D
ate of Application *

Street Address *

City *   **State** *
                                                                            Zip Code *

Phone *
                                                                            E
mail Address *

Website (if applicable)

Do you have an Advisory Board and/or Steering Committee for this project? *
Yes   No

If yes, please upload a document listing each person and include brief bios. Please also indicate if there are any public officials serving on your board or if there are any business or family relationships. Please label Advisory Board as Attachment A.

Name of Project *

Briefly state your project's mission statement and/or purpose *

Briefly describe the service you provide, the client population you serve, and the geographic community you expect will benefit from your activities *

What is the date you anticipate funds will be available to open your project account? *

████████████ ████████ sponsors both short and long term projects. **Do you have an end date in mind?** *

○ Yes ○ No

Upload Articles of Incorporation or Bylaws (if applicable)

You do not need to have Articles of Incorporation or Bylaws to be accepted for sponsorship by ████. If you are legally incorporated, please attach your Articles of Incorporation and Bylaws. Please label Articles as Attachment B and Bylaws as Attachment C.

Does your project plan to become recognized as a nonprofit by the IRS by obtaining your own 501(c)(3) in the next five years? *

○ Yes ○ No ○ Maybe

Have you filed for tax-exempt status? *

○ Yes ○ No

Does your project have insurance? *

○ Yes ○ No

Will you be lobbying/electioneering? *

○ Yes ○ No

What is the anticipated annual revenue of the project? *

Do you expect to earn any unrelated business income through sale of product or services? *

○ Yes ○ No

How many check requests do you expect to submit per month? *

Describe the nature of the expenditures you anticipate making *

How many grants do you expect to submit per quarter? *

How many special events do you expect to hold each year? *

How many online donation transactions do you expect per month? *

Please upload a document describing fundraising activities to date and also outline fundraising goals for the future. Please label the Fundraising document as Attachment D. *

Will your project need to hire W2 employees? *

○ Yes ○ No

Will your project need to contract with outside vendors/consultants? *

○ Yes ○ No

Will your project need to utilize volunteers? *

○ Yes ○ No

How did you hear about us? *

Are you currently using another Fiscal Sponsor? *

○ **Yes** ○ **No**

Please also upload the following attachments with your application: Proposed 12-month budget outlining the income and expenses for the project.

Two personal letters of reference from individuals familiar with you, your work in the community, and your commitment to making a difference. Please label Letters of Reference as Attachment F. Optional: Please attach other documents that may be beneficial for our review. Please label Miscellaneous as Attachment G. *

■■■■■■ ■■■■■■■■ Community Foundation

Fiscal Sponsorship Application Form

Submission of this application implies that you have read, understand, and agree to the information provided about Fiscal Sponsorship with the ■■■■■■ ■■■■■■ *Community Foundation.*

Organization Information

1. Individual, organization, or group submitting request:

    - Name:
    _____

    - Street Address:
    _____

    - City/State/ZIP:
    _____

    - Phone:
    _____

    - Email:
    _____

    - Contact Person
    _____

2. For what period of time is GMCF being asked to serve as Fiscal Sponsor?

    Start date: _____ **End date:**
    _____

3. Has your group incorporated as a separate legal entity? (Attach relevant correspondence.) Yes   No

4. Does your program plan to obtain its own 501(c)(3) status recognized as "nonprofit" by the IRS? Yes   No

If no, why not?

If yes, what has been done in preparation for securing 501(c)(3) status?

5. Does your program have liability insurance?
    - Circle one. Yes   No

6. Does your group have Bylaws?
    - Circle one. If yes, attach a copy. Yes   No

7. Do your plans include an endowment-building component to assure long-term stability.
    - Yes   No

Project Description

1. What are the goals of this project?

2. Who does the project serve?

3. What geographic area will the project serve?

4. How many people will benefit from the project and when?

5. What are the measureable outcomes of the project?

6. How do your goals relate to the purposes of the ▮▮▮▮▮ Community Foundation?

7. What criteria will guide the grant making from the fund?

8. Who is serving on the Advisory or Steering Committee for this project? (Attach list.)

9. What other groups or organizations are involved in this effort?

Services Requested from the ▇▇▇▇ ▇▇▇▇▇▇ Community Foundation

1. How many contributors do you expect to have and how much money do you anticipate being contributed to this fund **in the first year**? #_____ $

2. How many contributors do you expect to have and how much money do you anticipate being contributed **over the life** of the fund? #_____ $

3. When do you expect the first contribution to be made (mo/yr)?

4. Please attach your operating budget. How many receipts for expenses or requests for grants from the fund do you think ▇▇ will be asked to process? _____ per month or _____ per year?

5. When do you expect to request ▇▇ to pay the first expense or grant(mo/yr)?

6. Who will submit invoices or requests for grants to ▇▇ for payment from the fund, and why does that person or persons have this authority?

7. If ▇▇ does not serve as Fiscal Sponsor for this effort, please indicate which other organization could be likely candidates to do so, and your reasons for not making this request to them.

▇▇ will accept "pass-thru" funds in order to help donors achieve their philanthropic goals. These funds which promote or support the general charitable good of the community are established as a service of the Foundation. **An additional administrative fee of 1% or $10, whichever is greater, will be**

charged per distribution request *(checks written from the fund) for expendable or pass-thru contributions.* ***This fee is in addition to the 1% Annual Administration Fee described above.***

If it agrees to serve as your Fiscal Sponsor, ▮ must ensure that the outcomes and methods of your program are charitable. By signing this request, you are agreeing to abide by ▮ policies, including the fundraising and grant making policies; to provide ▮ with minutes of meetings, if requested; and to respond in writing to periodic questions from the ▮ regarding the activities of your program.

Before accepting an application for Fiscal Sponsorship, ▮ must be assured that appropriate plans are in place. Please attach a copy of your plans and indicate the strategies you will be using to secure assets for this fund.

Signature
Date

Fiscal Sponsorship Application Checklist

- ❏ Completed and signed application form
- ❏ Articles of Incorporation
- ❏ Bylaws
- ❏ IRS determination letter
- ❏ Fundraising plan
- ❏ Operating budget

Fiscal Sponsorship Application

████████ ████████, Inc. dba ████ ████ ████ ████ (████) is a non-profit organization as determined by the IRS under code 501(c)3. ████ is also a registered New York State charity.

DIRECTOR AND CONTACT INFORMATION			
PROJECT DIRECTOR (person who is fiscally responsible for this project)			
AFFILIATION			
ADDRESS			
CITY	STATE		ZIP/POSTAL
COUNTRY			
DAY PHONE	EVENING PHONE		FAX NUMBER
EMAIL			
PROJECT INFORMATION			
PROJECT TITLE			
ESTIMATED TOTAL BUDGET			
ESTIMATED PROJECT DURATION (beginning month and year to ending month and year)	FROM (month/year)		TO (month/year)
DATE OF THIS APPLICATION			

PROJECT DESCRITION (50 words or less)

ITEMS TO SUBMIT WITH THIS APPLICATION:

- A sample proposal or treatment for the production
- Itemized project budget

ITEMS TO SUBMIT WITH THIS APPLICATION, IF AVAILABLE:

- Proposed crew list
- A sample of work representative of the project

APPLICATATION PAYMENT

An application fee of $25.00 must be submitted with this application unless the project applicant has a ▮ individual artist application for the project that is still pending approval (check the box below that applies).

☐ Project applicant has a pending ▮ individual artist application for this project ☐ Application fee of $25.00 is enclosed

PAYMENT METHOD

☐ Check enclosed

☐ Visa   ☐ MasterCard   ☐ Discover   ☐ American Express Card Number

Expiration Date: _____ / _____ mm/yy

I authorize ▮, dba ▮ to charge the amount of $25.00 to my credit card

Card Member Signature:

Date:

Send your completed application to:

FISCAL SPONSORSHIP
PROGRAM ███████

███████

NEW YORK, NY ███████

Program Description

In accordance with its mission, ▇ serves as a Fiscal Sponsor of independent film and electronic media productions, as well as artistic, educational and cultural projects emphasizing the issues of people, groups, and nations outside of the economic mainstream.

▇▇▇▇ is a non-profit organization as determined by the IRS under code 501(c)3. It is also a registered New York State Charity. Under the ▇ Fiscal Sponsorship program, ▇ acts as an umbrella agency for your project, allowing the project to share some of the benefits of non-profit status that include:

- Tax deductible donations to your project from individuals and other entities that may be able to benefit from the tax deduction.

- Eligibility for funding from entities, such as foundations, government agencies, and other parties that may only provide grants and funding to non-profit entities.

As a project's umbrella agency, ▇ is the recipient of any funds donated or granted to the project. ▇ main- tains the funds in an account for the project. Account funds are disbursed to the project representative for the payment of legitimate project related expenses and services. As such, ▇ is responsible for ensuring that funds are used for project purposes and used in accordance with donors' and grantees' intent. This arrangement with ▇ can be as sole recipient of all project donations and grant funds or as recipient of only the funds associated with a specific grant. In either case, ▇ will issue the necessary project related 1099's in accordance with IRS guidelines.

If ▇ is to be sole recipient of all project funds, then ▇ is the exclusive agent for receiving and disbursing pro- ject related funds. In this arrangement, the project's representative is responsible to account for expenditures by providing ▇ receipts evidencing payment for project goods and services. ▇ will also provide the service of letters of thanks and acknowledgment to donors, ensure project representatives complete any required donation or grant related reports, and issue any required 1099's to the project's independent contractors and the project representative.

The Fiscal Sponsorship program does not provide any fund raising services, grant application services, or distribution services. Nor does acceptance into the Fiscal Sponsorship include ▆ distribution of the finished product. ▆ distribution requires a separate application, review, and approval. ▆ does not have any ownership or rights in the production at any time, nor is ▆ responsible for project content. The project's producers and/or directors are responsible for the content.

▆ charges an administrative fee of 5% of the project income (donations and grants) and 7% of grant amounts re- ceived from National Endowment for the Humanities and State Humanities Council grants. These amounts cover the expenses of ▆s services to maintain an accounting of donations and grants, send acknowledgment letters to do- nors and grantees, reconcile project receipts with project cash disbursements, generate and file IRS 1099 forms, and other services TWN must perform as the umbrella agency for the project.

There is a $25 application fee for each project submitted for consideration for ▆ Fiscal Sponsorship. This fee is waived for ▆ individual artist applicants pending funding. Additional fees will be charged to individual projects
for specific services such as messengers, mailings, cash advances, etc. Fees charged against contributed income are based on a uniform sliding scale.

The completed application should be sent to:

Fiscal Sponsorship ▆
▆

Applications are usually processed within ten (10) business days. Upon approval of the project and payment of the application fee, the project representative will be mailed a formal contract for execution and return to TWN. Ques- tions about the program and application status should be directed to the Fiscal Sponsorship Officer at fiscal_sponsorship@▆.org.

Eligibility Requirements

- The project must be a documentary or fictional work about issues, people, countries, or groups that society treats or perceives as being outside of the economic mainstream.

- The project must be a non-commercial film, video, or multimedia work

- The project representative payee (the person responsible to receive funds and pay expenses) must be a U.S. citizen with a tax identification number (Social Security Number or Federal Employee ID number).

- The project cannot promote any racism, sexism, or hate toward any person or group of people.

- The project representative must demonstrate, through the Fiscal Sponsorship application, an ability to raise project funds and produce a work through completion.

The Foundation ███████ ███████

██ Fiscal Sponsorship Application

██████████████████ appreciates the opportunity to consider your application for Fiscal Sponsorship, reviewing your Project's purpose, goals, actions items, budget and fundraising plan. We strive to review all applications within 1 month of submission, however, this time frame is not guaranteed.

Steps to Apply for Fiscal Sponsorship

Complete the Fiscal Sponsorship Application

- Please check all eligibility requirements before starting the application.

What Happens Next?

- **Phase 1:** Reviewers may contact you directly with questions or feedback about your application during the review process.
- **Phase 2:** ██ receives your application, reviews it and contacts you to set up a phone screening to learn more about your Project, answer any of your questions about Fiscal Sponsorship with ██ and share IRS and/or governmental Fiscal Sponsorship guidelines.
- **Phase 3:** Your application will be submitted for final review (including legal and insurance assessment) to determine if ██ can extend Fiscal Sponsorship to your Project. This phase could

take up to three months, since the Fiscal Sponsorship committee may have additional questions or request additional documentation.
- **Phase 4:** Once your Project has been determined to be eligible for Fiscal Sponsorship:
    - Your Project's Fiscal Sponsorship administrative fee will be determined based on your Project's scope of work, budget and needs
    - You will work with directly with a ▮ team member in developing your Fiscal Sponsorship Agreement

- You will complete an online review of ■'s Project Services Handbook
- You will sign the Fiscal Sponsorship Agreement
- You will work directly with a ■ team member in reviewing the next steps to begin implementing your Project's scope of work

Questions About the Fiscal Sponsorship Process?

Reach out the ▓▓▓▓▓▓▓▓▓▓▓▓▓▓▓

FISCAL SPONSORSHIP APPLICATION

* Required Response

Fiscal Sponsorship Application Acknowledgment

I acknowledge that I have read the eligibility criteria for ■s Fiscal Sponsorship listed below . *

- Projects are not providing a duplication of community services
- Projects do not attempt to influence legislation as a substantial part of their activities
- Projects cannot participate in any campaign activity for or against political candidates
- Projects must not be organization or operated for the benefit of private interests
- No part of the Project's donations may inure to the benefit of any private shareholder or individual
- Projects fundraising activities are in compliance with fundraising

guidelines from the IRS and any federal, state, local laws and regulations that may affect these activities

- The project and any of its activities must not present unacceptable levels of liability for ▇ as determined by ▇'s legal consultants
- The project and any of its activities must fall within ▇'s current insurance coverage, as determined by ▇'s insurance broker
- The project and any of its activities cannot provide any child care/day care services
- Projects cannot built, renovate or repair any residential or commercial housing facilities.

PROJECT PRIMARY CONTACT INFORMATION

Project Primary Contact Name*

First   **Last**

Project Primary Contact Address*

Street Address Address Line 2

City   **State**
                                         ZipCode

Project Primary Contact Phone* Project Primary Contact Email*

SECONDARY PROJECT CONTACT INFORMATION

(cannot be related to the Primary Project Contact)

Project Secondary Contact Name*

First   **Last**

Project Secondary Contact Address*

Street Address Address Line 2

City   **State**
                                         ZipCode

Project Secondary Contact Phone* Project Secondary Contact Email*

PROJECT INFORMATION

What is the name of the Project for which you are seeking Fiscal Sponsorship? *

Where is the location of your Project i.e., where will activities take place? *

(Please provide geographic information)

If you have one, what is the website address of your Project?

If you have any other social media pages for your Project, please list them here.

Is your Project currently being fiscally sponsored by another organization? *

Yes ☐   No ☐

If yes, please describe*

Is your Project incorporated as any type of legal entity? *

Yes ☐   No ☐

If yes, please describe*

PURPOSE OF THE PROJECT

What is the charitable mission and purpose of your Project? *

(Please tell us what problem/challenge your Project seeks to solve. Please also tell us what the expected positive influences of your Project will be including how many people will benefit as a result of your work or any other benefit to the community?)

GOALS OF THE PROJECT

How does your Project seek to solve the challenge/problem? *

ACTION ITEMS FOR THE PROJECT

Please provide a list of current and/or proposed activities that your Project will engage to meet this community need. *Please be specific, realistic and as thorough as possible.* *

PROJECT BUDGET

Please attach a detailed line item of expenses and project income for your Project's 1st year. *

A Project budget must be included with your Fiscal Sponsorship Application.

PROJECT FUNDING PLANS

Do you currently have funding for your Project? *

Yes ☐   No ☐

If yes, please describe*

Where do you expect the funding to come from? (Please check all that apply) *

☐ **Individual donations**

☐ **Fundraising community events** ☐ **Foundation grants**

☐ **Governmental grants** ☐ **Corporate sponsorships** **Web page donation page**

☐ **Other**

If Other, please describe*

Do you currently have commitments for any of your funding*

Yes ☐   No ☐

If yes, please describe*

Do you currently have or expect to apply for any type of government funding *(city, county, state, federal)*? *

Yes ☐   No ☐

If yes, please describe*

ADDITIONAL PROJECT QUESTIONS

Does your Project currently or plan to work with independent contractors? *

Yes ☐   No ☐

If yes, please describe*

Do you currently have or intend to develop any significant intellectual property? *

Yes ☐   No ☐

If yes, please describe*

Is there anything else you would like to tell us about your Project that you feel we should know or understand? *

How did you hear about us? *

Sample Agreements

The ▬▬ Trust

Sample Fiscal Sponsor Agreement

The Fiscal Sponsor has determined that sponsorship of the Project would be consistent with its goals, and wishes to make arrangements with the Sponsored Organization for the implementation and operation of the Project.

1. The Fiscal Sponsor hereby agrees to sponsor the Project and to assume administrative, programmatic, financial, and legal responsibility for purposes of the requirements of funding organizations. The Sponsored Organization agrees to implement and operate the Project, in accordance with the terms of this agreement and with any requirements imposed by funding organizations.

2. The Project shall be operated in a manner consistent with the Fiscal Sponsor's tax-exempt status and as described in this agreement. No material changes in the purposes or activities of the Project shall be made without prior written permission of the Fiscal Sponsor and in accordance with any requirements imposed by funding organizations, nor shall the Sponsored Organization carry on activities or use funds in any way that jeopardizes the Fiscal Sponsor's tax-exempt status.

3. The Sponsored Organization shall not, and shall not permit the Project to, attempt to influence legislation or participate or intervene in any political campaign on behalf (or in opposition to) any candidate for public office or otherwise engage in the carrying on of propaganda (within the meaning of section 501(c)(3) of the Internal Revenue Code of 1986).

4. The Sponsored Organization will provide the Fiscal Sponsor with reports describing programs and services of the Project in accordance with the following schedule:

[add here]

5. The Sponsored Organization will provide all information and prepare all reports, including interim and final reports, required by funding organizations, with the Fiscal Sponsor's assistance and final approval.

6. On behalf of the Sponsored Organization, the Fiscal Sponsor will establish and operate for the use of the Project a designated account ("Account") segregated on the Fiscal Sponsor's books. All amounts deposited into a Project's Account will be used in its support, less administrative charges, if any, and subject to the conditions set forth below.

7. The Fiscal Sponsor will disburse funds from the Account in the following manner:

    [add here. For example, as instructed in writing on properly filled-out Fiscal Sponsor vouchers accompanied by required documentation and only as authorized by this agreement.]

    Disbursements will be restricted to the support and implementation of the Project only.

8. The Sponsored Organization designates _____ (name) to act as authorizing official. The authorizing official shall act as principal coordinator of the Project's daily business with the Fiscal Sponsor, and shall have authority to sign disbursement requests [add additional authority, at no time should a person approve their own disbursement].

9. The Fiscal Sponsor and Sponsored Organization will maintain all financial records relating to the Project according to generally accepted accounting principles, retain records as long as required by law, and make records available to auditors as required by law.

10. The Fiscal Sponsor and the Sponsored Organization will reflect the activities of the Project, to the extent required, on their state and federal government tax returns and financial reports. All disbursements from an Account shall be treated as payments made to or on behalf of the Sponsored Organization to accomplish the purposes of the Project. The Sponsored Organization will provide the Fiscal Sponsor with proper documentation to accomplish this, including furnishing the Fiscal Sponsor with the Sponsored Organization's Federal Employer Identification Number.

11. **[[optional]** In consideration of the Fiscal Sponsor's agreement to sponsor the Project, and to cover the Fiscal Sponsor's expenses in connection with the Project as outlined above, the Project will pay the following fees, charges, and expenses:

(add here)

12. This agreement will be subject to review [set forth time period, e.g. annual], and will terminate if any of the following events occur:

[set add here. For example:

    a. The Fiscal Sponsor requests the Sponsored

Organization to cease activities that it deems might jeopardize its tax-exempt status and the Project fails to comply within a period of ten (10) days;

b. The Sponsored Organization fails to perform or observe any other covenant of this agreement, and this failure remains unremedied fifteen (15) days after notice in writing;

c. Upon expiration of four weeks after either the Sponsored Organization or the Fiscal Sponsor has given written notice of its intent to terminate the agreement.]

13. In the event this Agreement is terminated, the Fiscal Sponsor and Sponsored Organization will comply with any termination conditions imposed by funding organizations.

In witness whereof, the parties hereto have executed this Agreement on the day and year first written above.

Accepted for the Fiscal Sponsor:

_____
Authorized signer

_____
Date

For the Sponsored Organization:

_____
Authorized signer

_____
Date

 Network

SAMPLE

["RE-GRANT"] FISCAL SPONSORSHIP AGREEMENT

This Fiscal Sponsorship Agreement (this "Agreement") is entered into by and between _____ ("Sponsor"), and _____, ("Grantee"). This Agreement shall be effective as set out below at <u>Section 1</u>.

RECITALS

1. Sponsor has an Internal Revenue Service ("IRS") determination letter of qualification under Section 501(c)(3) of the Internal Revenue Code of 1986, as amended (the "Code") and is classified as a public charity under Code Sections 509(a)(1) and 170(b)(1)(A)(vi). Sponsor's purposes include _____;
2. The Grantee was formed as [**a Washington nonprofit corporation on** _____,] and does not have an IRS determination letter of qualification under Section 501(c)(3) of the Code. The Grantee's purposes include _____;
3. In furtherance of its charitable purposes, the Grantee operates a program (the "Sponsored Program") as described in the grant proposal ("Grant Proposal") which has been approved by Sponsor's board of directors and is attached hereto as <u>Exhibit A</u>;
4. The Grantee desires to have Sponsor act as its Fiscal Sponsor for the purpose of soliciting and receiving gifts, grants, contributions and other revenues (collectively, "donations") and distributing such funds to the Grantee, subject to Sponsor's oversight, to be used exclusively in support of the Sponsored Program;

5. Sponsor's board of directors has determined that the Sponsored Program furthers Sponsor's charitable goals and tax-exempt purposes. Sponsor's board of directors has authorized Sponsor to enter into a Fiscal Sponsorship agreement with the Grantee whereby Sponsor will receive donations on its own behalf and disburse such funds to the Grantee in support of the Sponsored Program, in accordance with the terms and conditions of this Agreement.

NOW, THEREFORE, the parties hereby agree as follows:

Effective Date. This Agreement shall become effective on _____, 20___.

Fiscal Sponsorship.

Sponsored Program Activities. The Grantee's officers shall act as principal coordinators of the Sponsored Program. Sponsor retains oversight authority to ensure that the funds disbursed by Sponsor to the Grantee in support of the Sponsored Program are used for their intended charitable purposes.

Receipt and Disbursement of Funds; Variance Power. In connection with its sponsorship of the Grantee, Sponsor agrees to receive donations that are designated as made in support of the Sponsored Program ("Sponsored Program Funds"). Sponsor anticipates granting Sponsored Program Funds to the Grantee, in furtherance of the Sponsored Program (less any administrative charge set out below). Upon request by the Grantee, Sponsor will disburse Sponsored Program Funds to the Grantee, assuming sufficient funds are available; provided, however, that in order to receive further disbursements the Grantee must be in compliance with all of its obligations under this Agreement, including specifically the reporting requirements set forth in <u>Section 5</u> hereto, and further provided that the date and amount of each disbursement of Sponsored Program Funds shall be within the discretion and control of

Sponsor. The Grantee assumes the risk that any funding source may exercise its discretion not to grant or not to appropriate funds to Sponsor for the support of the Sponsored Program. The parties intend that this Agreement be interpreted to provide Sponsor with variance powers necessary to enable Sponsor to treat the Sponsored Program Funds as Sponsor's assets while this Agreement is in effect. Sponsor, in its sole discretion, shall have the right to withhold, withdraw, or demand the immediate return of any Sponsored Program Funds if, in Sponsor's reasonable judgment, the Grantee materially breaches this Agreement or cannot accomplish the purposes of the Sponsored Program. Sponsor retains the right, in its sole discretion, to redirect the Sponsored Program Funds to a different charitable purpose or beneficiary if the purpose of the Sponsored Program becomes unnecessary, incapable of fulfillment, or inconsistent with the charitable needs of the community served by Sponsor.

Substantiation of Charitable Donations. Sponsor agrees that all Sponsored Program Funds will be reported for federal tax purposes as contributions to Sponsor and further agrees to acknowledge receipt of such Sponsored Program Funds in writing to donors, as required under federal tax law, and to furnish evidence of Sponsor's status as an organization qualified under Section 501(c)(3) of the Code to donors on request.

[Optional] Administrative Charge. Sponsor will retain an administrative charge to cover the costs associated with its management of the Sponsored Program Funds and other administrative expenses associated with this Agreement. This administrative charge shall be: _____ percent (__%) of the gross amount of the Sponsored Program Funds received by Sponsor annually. **[Optional:** Provided, however, that the administrative charge retained by Sponsor shall be no less than _____ dollars ($_____) per calendar quarter.**]**

Review by Sponsor. Sponsor and its representatives shall be given full access to the books, records, and senior management and financial personnel of the Grantee with respect to the Sponsored Program as Sponsor may reasonably request. Sponsor may, at its own expense, conduct an independent financial audit and/or program audit of the Grantee's books and records in relation to the charitable activities for which Sponsor has disbursed Sponsored Program Funds.

Financial Accounting and Reporting. Sponsor and the Grantee will maintain books and financial records for the Sponsored Program in accordance with generally accepted accounting principles, shall retain records as long as required by law and shall make records available to auditors as required by law. The Grantee will reflect the activities of the Sponsored Program, to the extent required, on its state and federal tax and information returns and financial reports. All disbursements from the Sponsored Program Funds shall be made payable to the Grantee.

Grantee Reporting Requirements.

Reports to Sponsor. The Grantee shall submit full and complete quarterly reports to Sponsor on the progress of the Sponsored Program. Such reports shall be due within thirty (30) days of the end of each calendar quarter, for so long as this Agreement remains in effect. Such reports shall describe the Grantee's use of the Sponsored Program Funds, compliance with the terms of all grants, and the progress made by the Grantee in accomplishing the purposes of the Sponsored Program.

Reports to Funding Sources. The Grantee will provide all information and prepare all reports, including interim and final reports, required by Sponsor to satisfy any funding sources, subject to Sponsor's final review and approval.

Notices. All notices or reports under this Agreement shall be addressed as follows:

If to Sponsor:

If to Grantee:

Such addresses may be changed by written notice or email notice given by such party to the other or by other form of notice agreed to by the parties.

Restrictions on Use of Sponsored Program Funds.

Tax-Exempt Purposes. The Grantee shall use the funds it receives from Sponsor solely for purposes of the Sponsored Program and shall not use such funds in any way that will jeopardize the tax-exempt status of Sponsor. The Grantee agrees to comply with any written request by Sponsor to cease activities that, in Sponsor's reasonable judgment, might jeopardize the tax-exempt status of Sponsor, and further agrees that Sponsor's obligation to make funds available to the Grantee is suspended in the event that it fails to comply with any such request.

Prohibited Activities. No portion of the Sponsored Program Funds shall be used in any attempt to influence legislation, **[except for lobbying expenditures approved in advance by Sponsor as set forth on the attached Exhibit A.]** No portion of the Sponsored Program Funds shall be used to participate or intervene in any political campaign on behalf of or in opposition to any candidate for public office, induce or encourage violations of law or public policy, cause private inurement or improper private benefit to occur, support terrorist activities, terrorist organizations or individuals who engage in or support terrorist activities, or take any other action inconsistent with qualification under Section 501(c)(3) of the Code.

Relationship of the Parties. Nothing in this Agreement shall constitute the naming of either party hereto as an agent or legal representative of the other party for any purpose whatsoever except as specifically and to the extent set forth herein. This Agreement shall not be deemed to create any relationship of agency, employment, partnership, or joint venture between the parties hereto and the Grantee shall make no such representation to anyone. It is the intention of the parties that all employees, contractors, and advisors for the Grantee will be employed or engaged directly by the Grantee and not by Sponsor.

Indemnification. The Grantee hereby irrevocably and unconditionally agrees, to the fullest extent permitted by law, to defend, indemnify, and hold harmless Sponsor, its officers, directors, trustees, employees and agents, from and against any and all claims, liabilities, losses and expenses (including reasonable attorneys' fees) directly, indirectly, wholly or partially arising from or in connection with any act or omission of the Grantee, its employees or agents, in applying for, accepting, expending or applying Sponsored Program Funds, or in carrying out the Sponsored Program, except to the extent that such claims, liabilities, losses or expenses arise from or in connection with any negligent act or omission of Sponsor, its officers, directors, trustees, employees or agents.

Fundraising. The Grantee *shall notify* Sponsor *(a) of all jurisdictions in which it would like* Sponsor *to solicit charitable contributions from the public in support of the* Sponsored Program; *and (b) if it intends to engage a commercial fundraiser to solicit charitable contributions from the public in support of the* Sponsored *Program*. All solicitations for the Sponsored Program shall be made in Sponsor's name. **All solicitation materials that use the name of** Sponsor **or its affiliates, including both written solicitation materials and scripts for oral solicitation communications, shall be subject to** Sponsor**'s advance approval.** The Grantee *shall comply with all laws and regulations concerning the solicitation of charitable contributions.* All original letters of inquiry and grant proposals *that use the name of* Sponsor *or any of its affiliates shall be subject to* Sponsor's *advance approval in its sole discretion and shall be signed by an authorized representative of* Sponsor. All grant agreements, pledges, or other commitments with funding sources to support the Sponsored Program *shall be subject to* Sponsor's *advance approval in its sole discretion and* shall be executed by Sponsor. The cost of any reports or other compliance measures required by such funding sources shall be borne by the Grantee.

Publicity. Any and all use of Sponsor's name in media communications and fundraising materials with respect to the Sponsored Program shall be subject to Sponsor's prior review and approval. The Grantee shall provide Sponsor with reasonable advance notice with respect to any proposed use of Sponsor's name in order to allow for such prior review.

Duration of Agreement. This Agreement shall remain in effect until the earliest of the following:

Grantee receives a determination letter from the IRS of its qualification under Section 501(c)(3) of the Code;

Sponsor or Grantee terminates this Agreement pursuant to the provisions of Section 13 below; or

_____, 20__.

Termination. Either party may terminate this Agreement without cause by giving thirty (30) days' written notice to the other party.

Disposition of Sponsored Program Funds in Termination. If there are any Sponsored Program Funds remaining after this Agreement has terminated, the following terms and conditions shall apply, subject to Sponsor's variance power set forth above at Section 2b:

If the Grantee has received a determination letter from the IRS of its qualification under Section 501(c)(3) of the Code, Sponsor shall transfer the balance of all Sponsored Program Funds, net of any liabilities incurred by Sponsor in connection with the Sponsored Program, to the Grantee for use in the Sponsored Program.

If the Grantee has entered into a written Fiscal Sponsorship agreement with another Fiscal Sponsor that has an IRS determination letter of qualification under Section 501(c)(3) of the Code, then Sponsor shall transfer the balance of any Sponsored Program Funds, net of any liabilities that Sponsor has incurred in connection with the Sponsored Program, to such new Fiscal Sponsor for use in the Sponsored Program.

In the event that the Grantee has not received an IRS determination letter from the IRS of qualification under Section 501(c)(3) of the Code or entered into a written Fiscal Sponsorship agreement with another Fiscal Sponsor that has an IRS determination letter of qualification under Section 501(c)(3) of the Code, Sponsor may allocate the Sponsored Program Funds in any manner consistent with applicable tax and charitable trust laws.

Miscellaneous Provisions.

Amendments. This Agreement may not be amended or modified, except in a writing signed by both parties hereto.

Dispute Resolution. In the event of a dispute under this Agreement, Sponsor and the Grantee shall make a good faith effort to resolve such dispute cooperatively before seeking to resolve any dispute by arbitration or otherwise proceeding with any remedy available at law or in equity.

Choice of Forum. The parties agree that the Superior Court of King County, Washington is the mandatory, exclusive venue for actions relating to this Agreement. The parties agree that King County is a convenient forum, and that all court proceedings shall be filed in King County and in no other forum.

Consent to Jurisdiction. For all purposes related to this Agreement, the parties hereby consent to personal jurisdiction in the state courts in and for the state of Washington.

Entire Agreement. This Agreement constitutes the entire agreement of the parties with respect to the subject matter hereof; it supersedes any prior agreement and understandings between the parties as to such matters, oral or written, all of which are hereby cancelled.

Governing Law. This Agreement shall be governed by and interpreted in accordance with the laws of the state of Washington.

Severability. Each provision of this Agreement shall be separately enforceable, and the invalidity of one provision shall not affect the validity or enforceability of any other provision.

Counterparts. This Agreement may be executed in counterparts, each of which shall be deemed an original and all of which together shall constitute one and the same instrument.

Attorneys' Fees. In the event of any controversy, claim, or dispute between the parties arising out of or related to this Agreement, or the alleged breach thereof, the prevailing party shall, in addition to any other relief, be entitled to recover its reasonable attorneys' fees and costs of sustaining its position.

Remainder of page intentionally left blank

SIGNATURE PAGE TO

FISCAL SPONSORSHIP AGREEMENT

Between

_____

And

_____

IN WITNESS WHEREOF, the parties have caused their duly authorized representatives to execute this Agreement effective as of the day and year set out in <u>Section 1</u> of this Agreement.

Sponsor: _____,

a [█████] nonprofit corporation]

Grantee:

_____

a [█] nonprofit corporation]

EXHIBIT A

APPROVED GRANT PROPOSAL

[If the Sponsored Program includes lobbying activities, this Grant Proposal must include a grant budget, specifying the total amount of the lobbying budget and the amount, if any, that will be used for grassroots lobbying.

▓▓▓▓▓▓▓ Alliance (CA)

Contract For

Fiscal Sponsorship Services

This is an agreement for Fiscal Sponsorship services, entered into between the ▓▓▓▓▓▓▓ Alliance (Alliance) and the _____ ("Project").

Recitals

The ▓▓▓▓▓▓▓ (Alliance) is a nonprofit corporation, exempt from federal tax under section 501(c)(3) of the Internal Revenue Code, as most recently amended. ▓▓▓▓▓▓▓ Alliance's mission is to protect and restore the natural environment of the ▓▓▓▓▓▓▓ for future generations while ensuring healthy and sustainable communities.

The _____ ("Project") is an [unincorporated association; or a coalition of organizations; or an independent nonprofit organization] with the mission of

_____

. Alliance is willing to receive tax-deductible charitable

contributions for the benefit and use of the Project. The Project,

with the administrative assistance of the Alliance, desires to use

these funds in order to implement the Project's purposes.

Agreement

By entering into this Agreement, the parties agree to the following terms and conditions:

1. <u>Receipt of funds</u>: The Alliance agrees to receive grants, contributions and gifts to be used for the Project, and to make those funds available to the Project, minus assessed administrative fees, as specified in this agreement.

2. <u>Administrative Fees</u>: To defray the expenses associated with administering the Project, the Project agrees to pay the Alliance an administrative fee of (5% for small groups 7% for larger – specific amount to be entered on individual agreement) on all income received including, but not limited to, grant income and contributions.

3. <u>Acknowledgments</u>: Alliance and Project agree that all grants, charitable contributions, and gifts that Alliance receives for the Project will be reported as contributions to the Alliance, as required by law. Alliance further agrees to acknowledge the receipt of any such grant, charitable contribution, or gift in writing, and to furnish evidence of its status as a tax-exempt organization under Section 501(c)(3) as requested, or as required by law. In its acknowledgement of gifts made on behalf of the Project, the Alliance will inform the donor that the contribution made will benefit the Project.

4. <u>Protection of tax-exempt status</u>: The Project agrees not to use funds received from the Alliance in any way that would jeopardize the tax-exempt status of the Alliance. The Project agrees to comply with any written request by the Alliance that it cease activities which might jeopardize the Alliance's tax status, and further agrees that the Alliance's obligation to make funds available to it is suspended in the event that it fails to comply with any such request. Any changes in the purpose for which grant funds are spent must be approved in writing by the Alliance before implementation. The Alliance retains the right, if the Project breaches this Agreement, or if the Project jeopardizes the Alliance's legal or tax status, to withhold, withdraw, or demand immediate return of grant funds.

5. <u>Notice to Project By Alliance</u>: The Alliance agrees to notify the Project of any change in its tax- exempt status.

6. <u>Use of funds</u>: The Alliance will allow the Project to make expenditures from funds collected by the Alliance to achieve the purposes of the Project. In no case will any such expenditure exceed total contributions for the Project received by the Alliance, and Alliance will not advance funds to the Project beyond those received by the Alliance. The Project agrees to use any and all funds received from the Alliance solely for legitimate expenses of the Project and fully to account to the Alliance for the disbursement of these funds. Prior to any such expenditure, the Alliance will obtain authorization from the Project to pay these expenses using the Project's funds.

7. <u>Financial accounting and reporting</u>: The Project will in all cases follow the Alliance's financial policies and

accounting procedures as established by the Alliance. Specifically, the Project will adopt the Alliance's fiscal year, which extends from July 1st through June 30th. The Alliance will maintain books and financial records for the Project in accordance with generally accepted accounting principles, and the Project's revenue and expenses shall be separately classed in the books of the Alliance. The Alliance will provide reports reflecting revenue and expenses to the Project on a monthly basis, within 30 days after the end of each month.

8. Budgeting: The Project will provide the Alliance with its annual budget at the beginning of each fiscal year.

9. Governance: Authority to manage the programmatic activities of the Project is delegated to the Project. Normally, the Project's Board will exercise that authority. Notwithstanding the forgoing, both Alliance and Project agree that the relationship established by this agreement is premised upon the mutual understanding of Alliance and Project that the goals and activities of both organizations will be compatible. In order to maintain such compatibility of goals and activities over time, Project agrees to inform Alliance of any new or changed activities contemplated by Project, and if Alliance determines that the programmatic activities of the Project are in fact inconsistent with the goals and activities of Alliance, Alliance shall draw this immediately to the attention of Project, and shall retain the right to terminate this agreement, pursuant to the provisions of Paragraph 14.

10. Fundraising: The Project may solicit gifts, contributions, and grants on behalf of the Alliance, and such gifts, contributions, and grants, if and when received, will be earmarked for the activities of the Project. The Project's

choice of funding sources to be approached and the text of the Project's letters of inquiry, grant applications, and other fundraising materials are subject to approval by the Alliance. The Alliance's Executive Director must co-sign all original letters of inquiry, grant proposals, and grant agreements. All grant agreements, pledges, or other commitments with funding sources to support the Project shall be executed by the Alliance. The cost of any reports or other compliance measures required by such funding sources shall be borne by the Project. The Alliance's Executive Director must be copied at least one week in advance on all progress and final report submissions. The Alliance shall be responsible for the processing and acknowledgment of all monies received for the project, which shall be reported as the income of the Alliance for both tax purposes and for purposes of the Alliance's financial statements. Grants involving government or public agency monies have substantial reporting and auditing requirements; therefore, if the Project desires to apply for government or public agency grants, the Project must get advance approval to do so from the Alliance's Executive Director.

11. Renewal of this agreement: If both the Alliance and Project desire to do so, this agreement may be renewed annually, and the annual term of any such renewal shall be coincident with Alliance's fiscal year.

12. Termination: Either party may terminate this Agreement by giving 90 days' written notice to the other party.

13. Disposition of Assets and Liabilities: If either party terminates this agreement, any funds collected on

behalf of the Project, and remaining in the possession of the Alliance at the time of termination, shall be disposed of according to existing written agreements with funding sources. If the Project continues beyond the term of this agreement, funds and assets not covered by existing written agreements with funding sources may be transferred to another nonprofit corporation (the Successor) that is tax-exempt under IRC Section 501(c)(3) and that is not classified as a private foundation under Section 509(a). The Successor must be willing and able to sponsor the Project. The Successor must be approved in writing by the Alliance and the Project by the end of the 90-day period for written notice of termination. If a Successor is found, the balance of assets not covered by existing agreements with funding sources held by the Alliance for the Project, together with any other assets held or liabilities incurred by the Alliance in connection with the Project, shall be transferred to the Successor at the end of the 90-day period of written notice of termination or any extension thereof, subject to the approval of any third parties (including funding sources) that may be required. If the Project has formed a new organization qualified to be a Successor as set forth in this Paragraph, such organization shall be eligible to receive all such assets and liabilities so long as such organization has received a determination letter from the Internal Revenue Service which states the new organization is exempt from federal tax under section 501(c)(3) of the Internal Revenue Code no later than the end of the 90-day period of written notice of termination or any extension thereof. If no Successor is found by the end of the 90-day period of written notice of termination, the Alliance may allocate the Project's assets and liabilities in any manner consistent with applicable tax and charitable trust laws and other obligations.

The time period covered by this agreement is from July 1, 2009 to June 30, 2010, and the agreement will terminate on the date last specified, unless it is either renewed as specified in Paragraph 13, or is terminated with 90 days written notice by either the Alliance or the Project, as provided in Paragraph 14.

By signing below, both parties hereby execute this Agreement according to its terms, and the individuals signing on behalf of the Alliance and the Project, by signing this Agreement, certify that they are legally empowered and authorized to do so on behalf of the Alliance and the Project, respectively.

Alliance: **Project:**

█████ █████ Association (CT)

Memorandum of Understanding between █████████ Association and XYZ ████████ regarding ████████ serving as a fiscal agent for activities associated with the XYZ River Watershed

updated on May 2nd 2008 to honor current working agreements

The ████████████████████████████ Association (hereafter '██A') will serve as a 501(c)3 nonprofit fiscal agent for Ms. _____ (hereafter 'Ms. _____') in the following ways:

██ will not represent that it is an "employer" of Ms. _____.

██ is a 501(c)3 nonprofit organization serving as a fiscal agent to support Blank River watershed activities;

██ will receive funding raised through grants, individual or corporate donations, or fee for service activities that will be allocated to specific efforts to protect, restore, and conduct education and outreach activities regarding the Blank River Watershed;

██ will accurately acknowledge work performed by Ms. _____ in project related public announcements;

██ will recognize Ms. _____ as the Project Director of the Blank ██ Revitalization Initiative by involving her in related budget and administrative decisions for project work that she has generated, including grant funding, project fees and/or other gifts;

██ will pay invoices submitted by ██_____ and approved by ██ in a timely fashion (typically within two (2) weeks of receipt) for activities in the Blank River Watershed with funding raised specific to Blank River Watershed initiatives;

■ will pay ■_____the flat fee or hourly rate as listed in the project work and grant proposals, (pending project work and grants submitted at this time include: *itemized list of ongoing grant projects*);

■ will realize a reasonable, nominal fee to cover administrative and/or program expenses associated with managing funds, contracting/subcontracting, invoicing, grant writing, or distributing funds on behalf of Blank ■ activities. Any fees will be negotiated with ■ in advance of being assessed.

■___will serve as a contractor for ■ in the following ways:

Ms. _____ will not represent that she is an "employee" ■■■■■■■■■■■■.

_____ is working with ■ as an independent contractor to fulfill obligations incurred by grants or contracts focused on Blank River ■■■■■■■ activities;

Ms. _____ can raise funding for specific Blank ■ pre-approved by the Executive Director of the ■ on behalf of its Board of Directors;

Ms. _____ can submit invoices to ▮ and expect payment in a timely fashion (typically within two (2) weeks of receipt) for pre-approved activities to protect, restore, and conduct education and outreach activities regarding the Blank River Watershed;

Ms. _____ will negotiate with ▮ to determine administrative and/or program expenses incurred through managing funds, contracting/subcontracting, invoicing, grant writing, or distributing funds on behalf of Blank River Watershed activities. Fees will be assessed only after negotiation with Ms. _____.

Agreed to by _____

Date

Agreed to by _____
▮▮▮▮▮▮▮▮▮▮▮▮ Association
Date

Other Fiscal Sponsorship Websites and resources

https://www.fiscalsponsors.org/

https://fiscalsponsordirectory.org/

https://www.socialimpactcommons.org/